Beyond Appearances

THE JEWISH PUBLICATION SOCIETY

1888-1988

Aryeh Wineman

Beyond Appearances

Stories from the Kabbalistic Ethical Writings

The Jewish Publication Society
Philadelphia   New York   Jerusalem
5748   1988

Copyright © 1988 by Aryeh Wineman
First edition   All rights reserved
Manufactured in the United States of America

Library of Congress Cataloging in Publication Data
Wineman, Aryeh.
  Beyond appearances.

  Includes index.
  1. Legends, Jewish.   2. Parables, Jewish.
  3. Exempla, Jewish.   4. Luria,
Isaac ben Solomon, 1534–1572—Legends.   5. Cabala.
6. Judaism—Israel—Tsefat.   7. Tsefat (Israel)—Religious
life and customs.   I. Title.
BM530.W56 1988   296.1'9   87–26183
ISBN 0-8276-0307-X

Designed by Tracy Baldwin

In connection with the preparation of this volume, I am grateful for having been able to draw upon the library resources of Yale University, the Jewish Theological Seminary, the Bodleian Collection at Oxford, the National Library located at the Hebrew University, Jerusalem, and the collection housed at the Schocken Institute, also in Jerusalem. I am especially appreciative for a research stipend received from the National Endowment for the Humanities in the summer of 1983, which enabled me to further my research on this subject at Oxford and in Jerusalem. Without that grant I could never have completed this project.

I want to express my appreciation to Sheila F. Segal, editor-in-chief, and to Barbara Spector, managing editor, respectively, of the Jewish Publication Society, for their interest in this project and for their valuable suggestions and assistance in preparing this book for publication.

A. W.

לדבורה, בתפילה לרפואתה

Contents

Contents

"But the Lord said to Samuel,
'Pay no attention to his appearance or his
stature . . . for things are not as man sees
them; a person sees only what is visible, but
the Lord sees into the heart.' "

1 Samuel 16:7

Beyond Appearances

Introduction

One finds Jewish stories recorded through the centuries in many different kinds of books. In most of these volumes storytelling was not an end in itself but, rather, a vehicle for outlining a way of life and a particular world view. The stories in this collection represent a highly significant—though today little known—body of writings whose authors were rooted in the spiritual world of Jewish mysticism, or Kabbalah. To one degree or another, they attempted to translate that world, its insights and values, into a form that could reach out to large numbers of Jews and have an impact on their daily lives. Although most of these works were written in various places and over several centuries, their spiritual roots are to be found in the sixteenth century, in the small Upper Galilee town of Safed, which, following the expulsion of the Jews from Spain and Portugal, became a unique center of Jewish learning and of Kabbalah in particular. Its influence ultimately touched much of the rest of the Jewish world, in effect re-creating that world in its own image.

Perched on a mountaintop in modern Israel, Safed is today the site of a renowned artists' colony. Its painters draw inspiration from both the haunting landscape and the memories and overtones of Jewish mysticism so closely associated with the town's past. Still standing in the oldest part of Safed are synagogues that date back, in some cases, to the sixteenth century and that bear the names of some of the great rabbis of that era. The town faces Mount Meron to the west and lies almost in its shadow. At the foot of the peak is the burial site traditionally ascribed to the second-century sage Rabbi Simeon bar Yohai and his son Eleazar. The Kabbalists of the time believed that Bar Yohai was the author of the Zohar, the classic text of Jewish mystic teaching.

During the 1500s and long afterward, until the beginning of our own century, Safed was part of the Ottoman Empire, which provided a haven for Jews expelled from Spain and Portugal during the last decade of the fifteenth century. One cannot understand Safed apart from the trauma of the expulsion of Jews from a land in which they had roots going back close to a thousand years. In Safed, older mystic traditions and messianic hopes met and in meeting became transformed. Other factors contributing to the growth of a Jewish community in Safed were the development of a thriving textile manufacturing center, the friendliness of local officials, and an old tradition that the Messiah would first appear in the Galilee.[1]

In his famous essay on Safed, published shortly after the turn of this century, Solomon Schechter wrote that "the Safed of the sixteenth century must have been a veritable Paradise on earth to any man with a tendency toward intellectual pursuits."[2] Among its small population were numbered legal scholars such as Jacob Berab, Moses de Trani, and Joseph Caro, author of the famous code of Jewish law, the *Shulḥan arukh.* Also to be found in Safed were Solomon Alkabez, a mystic thinker remembered as the poet of *Lekha Dodi,* which is recited to this day in greeting the Sabbath, and Moses Cordovero, the leading teacher of Kabbalah until Isaac Luria ultimately superseded him in influence. One can add the names of Moses Alshekh, the noted preacher and commentator, and Moses de Vidas and Eleazer Azikri, writers of ethical texts. These were some of the many luminaries in what was, even by the standards of the times, but a small town.

But apart from its leading personalities and books, sixteenth-century Safed is known for the particular mode of spirituality that took root and blossomed there, a spiritual revival characterized by rituals and ascetic practices that cultivated purity of heart and humility before the omnipresent God. The Kabbalists' intense devotion to the life of piety and to the study of Torah grew from a sense of the need for a wholehearted turning to God, echoing, as a counterresponse, the apostasizing tendencies (even if only because of external pressure) of many Jews of Spain and Portugal, where many of the Jews of Safed had their family roots.

Again in the words of Solomon Schechter, "Luria, in common with other mystics, succeeded in spiritualizing the whole life of man . . ."[3] That mode of spirituality was marked both by an "austere morality"[4] and by an emphatic social ethic rooted in the love of God and the aspiration to bring wholeness and healing to all of existence, which is painfully estranged from itself. This aspiration is given particular expression in Lurianic Kabbalah. The people of Israel, the entire world, even the Divinity suffer the pangs of exile. The supreme task is thus defined as one of restoring a lost oneness and wholeness. By fulfilling the mitzvot, the commandments of Torah, with true devotion and a purity of intent, the Jews of Safed believed they held the keys to unlocking and hastening divine redemption. This conviction contained within itself a sense of terror at the possibility of failure.

Over the course of time, sixteenth-century Safed, with its small population, came to influence Jews virtually wherever they lived, leaving its imprint upon world Jewry as a whole, both through the spread of the complex theories of Lurianic Kabbalah and through the popular ethical texts that outlined the devout life in terms accessible to vast numbers of Jews. Many of these books date from the seventeenth and even the eighteenth and nineteenth centuries and were written in other places—in Smyrna or Istanbul, in Amsterdam and Frankfurt and Baghdad—but they all bear the stamp of that idiom of spirituality that flourished in sixteenth-century Safed.

The authors of these ethical texts—while continuing much earlier traditions of Jewish ethical literature—also color those same traditions with the idiom of their own particular world view. In speaking of Jewish ethical literature, it is necessary to bear in mind that the concept of *musar* (ethics) in traditional Jewish sources refers not to an essentially autonomous or separate realm of human relationships but, rather, to the totality of the Jew's relationship with God. This relationship colors every aspect of one's life, including one's relationship with one's fellow and with oneself. The kabbalistic ethical writings, in particular, share in spelling out the ideal of the Hasid: one whose love for God is whole and is expressed throughout the entirety of his life.

These pietistic writings do not contain theoretical formulations of mystical teaching. Rather, they tend to define that teaching in terms of a concrete way of life and complex of values. Hence it was natural that some of the authors would use stories for their didactic purposes: interweaving into their discourses and discussions various forms of the genre, including parables, legends, moral tales, and anecdotes. Some of those stories are taken over largely intact from earlier sources; in others, the reader may still recognize earlier materials, motifs, or story types that have been remolded, sometimes radically reworked, in the light of the particular ethos of the period in which this literature blossomed. In such cases, the stories themselves have interesting histories. A reading of the stories from such texts requires, whenever possible, ascertaining the kinds of questions or issues that the story, in its own way, attempts to address.

Although the narratives found in this body of writings are of various types, they share a particular set of qualities, an ambience quite their own. Particular overtones emerge and are heard in many different stories of this milieu. Reading those stories in light of the larger corpus of the Jewish tale and legend, one might consider the analogy of an optometrist testing a patient's eyesight for glasses, throwing one lens over another to alter the field of vision. In a similar manner, the folk materials or literary sources from which these works drew are often altered to mirror underlying attitudes and values basic to the spirit that permeated the world of Safed. Let us try to define some of those lenses that together constitute the ethos voiced in these stories.

Common to many of these writings is a strong note of paradox, one of those basic overtones heard in the narratives. Things are not necessarily as they appear to be or as we are accustomed to perceiving or regarding them. Truth, in other words, is not to be equated with the world as it appears to the human eye. Each person bears a truth about himself to which others may be blind, a truth that is perhaps hidden from the world or even from that person himself. A scholar might have a grave moral blemish, whereas the seemingly insignificant and even unlearned person might do something that renders him spiritually precious. These stories reflect a sense of reality in which the unexpected can always occur, shattering society's assumptions and judgments.

Various stories, including some drawn from earlier sources, express in explicit or implicit terms the polarity between the Hakham, the man of learning, and the Hasid, the devout person, learned or unlearned, whose qualities are not contingent upon intellectual attainment. Some of the tales may even have originated as subtle expressions of protest on the part of the basically unlearned, socially marginal Jew against those of great status—those associated with the life and institutions of intense talmudic study. Indeed, these same stories appealed to the mystical authors for related reasons. While acknowledging that the attainments of learning are accessible to only a portion of the population, they believed that the gates to a life of piety are nevertheless open to every Jew, irrespective of knowledge, family background, or economic circumstances—and this body of writings addresses itself to the masses of Jews. In addition, as much as the study of Torah is a value extolled in this literature, ultimately the values of the Hasid take precedence over those of learning. One who has excelled in Torah study but lacks inner devoutness and spirituality has actually failed to grasp the very meaning of Torah. His learning is an empty shell, despite the honors society accords him. In its more radical expressions, voiced in some of the stories, this polarity extends even to the Jew who lacks familiarity with the most basic norms of religious observance but whose inner intent, it is disclosed, impresses God Himself.

It follows that one never knows the true worth or importance of a person. A beggar who comes to one's door might be the prophet Elijah or the patriarch Abraham appearing in disguise. A poor person, ignored by those around him, might ultimately have the power of life and death over those highly respected in his society. There is, then, no insignificant person, for each one might have a crucial role in the transcendent network of events that influence our world. The turning point in some of these stories is a radical reevaluation of the way a particular individual is perceived by others.

Similarly, these stories challenge the assumption that we can judge the importance of a deed, for human acts that appear insignificant may be the very ones that have the greatest impact. There is, in fact, no insignificant deed, whether it be a righteous or pious act or a transgression. Each human act, including even unintentional deeds, can have far-reaching consequences. These stories often convey a sense that our conventional categories of great and small, of important and insignificant, can be grossly misleading. The real truth of things, we are told, can vary surprisingly from commonly accepted norms. And, as spelled out in kabbalistic thought, the consequences of a deed can seriously affect not only the individual and his or her immediate environment but also all of the world, all of being, the seen and the unseen, the physical and the divine. In terms of the ideology of Lurianic Kabbalah in particular, a human deed, seemingly great or small, can promote either renewed wholeness or prolonged and more aggravating exile and alienation throughout the cosmos.

The anxiety concerning the grave and the drastic consequences of a misdeed is not unrelated to a sense of bewilderment and dread, of utter astonishment and fright that permeates story after story emerging from this milieu. In most cases, shock gives way to relief as the iniquity or the hidden misdeed—often hidden even to the person responsible for it—is corrected. The change of mood, from dismay to relief, accompanies the fact of *tikkun,* the act of mending the wrong done and of repairing its spiritual impact both upon the individual's soul and upon the higher worlds, removing the stain of sin that blemishes the soul and all of being. In rarer instances, though—and these possess remarkable dramatic power—the element of disquiet knows no relief; it continues to the very end or emerges only at the conclusion of the story. In such cases the principle of *tikkun* does not operate, and the reader is left with a profound sense of disappointment or of the inalterability of negative consequences.

Although a number of personalities are included in this literature, central to it is the Ari (Rabbi Isaac ben Solomon Ashkenazi Luria, 1534–1572). This great teacher, who resided in Safed for only the last two years of his life, entrusted to his small group of students his daring views of the cosmos and the divine[5] and became the subject of whole collections of legends. It has even been suggested that those legends that made their way to other lands paved the way for the later acceptance of his esoteric teaching, making Lurianic Kabbalah the predominant ideology of the Jewish world for almost two centuries.[6] The Ari legends portray Luria as possessing virtually infinite knowledge, cognitive powers that far exceed human norms and that enable him to reveal a person's hidden deeds, including even things hidden to that person himself. Grasping worldly happenings in the light of a transcendent perspective, he knows the real significance of an act; he perceives and discloses the inner connections between happenings and situations; and his wondrous knowledge extends even to one's actions in previous lives. Such legends sometimes posit examples of bizarre behavior or occurrences, which later make sense in terms of what is revealed by his supernatural knowledge. Some of the stories attribute this special knowledge to others as well, including the anonymous Hasid, who merits it by virtue of his spiritual qualities.

It is curious that many other legendary motifs conventionally associated with the figure of the holy man are absent in the Ari legends, or at least in those that appear to have emerged close to his lifetime within his circle of followers—leaving only the theme of wondrous knowledge as a persistent feature. Perhaps this is because the role of the Ari in these legends is to break through the boundaries of human perception and knowledge in order to arrive at a more complete truth about people and things. Through his wondrous knowledge, the Ari is able to bring the hidden, or even the unknown, to the realm of the knowable, and in so doing he makes it accessible to *tikkun*. That which is known can be repaired;

but that which remains hidden cannot be mended or rectified and remains as an obstacle to messianic redemption. As one of the pillars of the Ari's theosophic teachings, the principle of *tikkun* leads to messianic fulfillment, shattering both the historical exile of Israel and the greater cosmic exile affecting the Divine itself. The Ari of the legends, through his supernatural cognitive capacities, makes *tikkun* a possibility in human life. The same legends might impress today's readers as breathing a very modern—or postmodern—sense of the human mind and will, as involving much more than the conscious or rational mind. Hence not only small deeds or misdeeds but also those acts quite beyond the realm of conscious intent and awareness are significant and even crucial.

While the Ari is usually the hero of these legends, one finds within the corpus a subgenre that points precisely to his failure to bring redemption: The legend of the holy man is transformed into an anti-tale.[7] The lofty and unbounded expectations of his time confront the fact of an unredeemed world, a world still in the throes of exile; the idealized world of the legendary hero confronts a historical reality that negates it. Whereas the Ari of the legends accomplished *tikkun* on the level of the individual, he could not achieve the fullness of *tikkun*—the end of dislocation on national, cosmic, and divine levels. These legends end in a mood of utter despair, and they breathe a tragic irony that is usually found in writers closer to our own time, such as M. J. Berdyczewski and Franz Kafka. One can speculate that such legends emerged in response to the death of the Ari in 1572, at a time when many looked upon him as a messianic figure and, on the basis of the interpretation of biblical verses, even identified the year 1575 as the appointed time of messianic fulfillment.[8]

The failure in those legends is not that of the Ari but, more properly, that of his followers. They are unable to stand the test of a wholehearted readiness for *tikkun*. Their failing, then, consists largely in the inability to subdue their mundane impulses and considerations in the face of a potentially redemptive moment; they are unable to enter completely and unanimously into the nature of the sacred. The legends of this type evoke a sense of vast distance separating the Ari even from the restricted circle of his close students, so that the master himself emerges as a solitary figure. These stories convey his anxiety that the Jews of Safed were still very distant from being able to hasten messianic redemption through commitment to a life of *tikkun*—notwithstanding the community's self-image to the contrary.

9

One lens coloring some of these stories is the polarity between exile and restlessness, on one hand, and rest, on the other—a polarity present on some level in several of the narratives. The note of rest in such a story connotes redemption and an end to the wandering and exile that Jews felt ever more poignantly following their expulsion from the Iberian Peninsula. Wandering and restlessness in these tales and legends produce overtones of Jewish historical experience—and also of the exile within God and hence within all existence, as claimed in Lurianic Kabbalah. Even stories originating in a much earlier period now convey, in the polarity of rest and unrest, the additional dimension of redemption and the pain of ongoing exile.

As mentioned previously, one finds in these stories much older motifs and narrative patterns that have undergone decided metamorphosis as they come to be colored or remolded by the ethos of sixteenth-century Safed. In some of the most intriguing cases, a comparison of such stories with their likely sources, or with stories that stand in the background of the narratives, points to the fashioning of earlier materials to voice themes such as the exile of the Divine Presence, the suffering within the divine realm itself, along with the belief, expressed in the rituals that emerged largely in Safed,[9] that the Jew's intense empathy with the Shekhinah, the Divine Presence, in Her exile can serve to destroy the very force of exile itself. Alongside the transformation of earlier narrative traditions, the reader also notes subtle variations in the story line, which suggest that now the study of Kabbalah is no longer reserved for a spiritual and intellectual elite but is to be made accessible to large numbers of Jews as a means of furthering the process of *tikkun* and redemption. The highly creative reworking of earlier materials points to a significant facet of the narrative art of these stories.

Looking at them as a whole, the legends, the moral tales, and the parables, one essential thrust appears to predominate: the disclosure of what is hidden. The typical Ari legend brings the concealed, or simply the unknown, to the level of the known. The stories dealing with metempsychosis, the transmigration of souls, radically expand the realm of knowledge by revealing facts concerning a person's larger biography, that is, a person's prior lives. Thus the paradoxical moral tale might reevaluate society's perception of a person in some crucial way because, again: Things are not as they appear to be, and they are more than they appear to be. In this respect, these stories are in consonance with a deeper strain essential to the nature of Jewish mysticism: the disclosure of that which is hidden, unknown, and, paradoxically, even unknowable.

It should therefore be clear that we are dealing with a unique chapter in the history of the Jewish story, a chapter that has not hitherto been the focus or subject of concentrated literary examination. Neither has it been made readily available to the wider public.

Among the stories in this collection are three basic types: legends, moral tales, and parables. One might make the claim that the mythic dimension and ambience of Kabbalah allowed for the rebirth of the Jewish legendary story with a degree of narrative power and imaginative thrust that far exceeded that of the legends found in classical and rabbinic lore. Many of the legends, as we have noted, are about the Ari and emphasize his quality of wondrous knowledge. By contrast, the moral tales in this collection, while often quite similar to the legends, do not relate to a historical figure or known holy man. Their real hero is not a specific individual but, rather, the archetypical figure of the Hasid, who personifies through his deeds and qualities the values central to the teachings of this body of ethical writings. The third category of stories, the parables, tends to exemplify a point or theme in terms of a realm of experience often alien to it. Hence these parables might illuminate the values of the spiritual life by means of projected situations drawn even from the most worldly of settings.

Although these stories from the kabbalistic ethical texts and kindred sources draw frequently from the stuff of folktales—and some may have originally been transmitted orally—it must be remembered that they are literary creations embedded in literary sources by known or anonymous authors. And many of them display remarkable narrative craftsmanship. Some are highly polished gems, multifaceted in their display of creative association, subtlety, and insight. This is especially the case in several of the stories from *Hemdat yamim,* an anonymous eighteenth-century text that represents the moderate strand of the Sabbatean messianic movement. The latter, even in its heresy, shared the pietistic and ascetic mood of Lurianic Kabbalah, from which it grew.

The reader familiar with the Jewish story of later times will recognize in this collection qualities that took on renewed life, albeit in somewhat different soil, in the tales of the hidden righteous or saintly personalities who sustain the world, in the polemical tales that pit the later Hasid against the learned rabbi whose knowledge lacks inner fire, as well as in the tragic irony of some modern writers. In particular, the stories in this collection, which give voice to the world of Kabbalah from the sixteenth through the eighteenth centuries, provide a background for the Hasidic stories that were first published in the early nineteenth century. They provide evidence that the later Hasidic story did not emerge in a vacuum but grew from earlier roots.[10]

If one views Kabbalah not only as a network of ideas but also as a total culture informed by a particular mind-set, then the story is one way to approach the world of Kabbalah. The reader will find in these stories an unusual interplay of narrative imagination and spirituality that has enriched our religious and cultural legacy.[11]

1. Zohar 1:119a; 2: 7b, 9a, 220a.

2. Solomon Schechter, "Safed in the Sixteenth Century: A City of Legists and Mystics," *Studies in Judaism: Second Series* (Philadelphia, 1908), 250.

3. *Ibid.*, p. 278.

4. *Ibid.*, p. 281.

5. Gershom Scholem, *Major Trends in Jewish Mysticism* (New York, 1946), 244–286.

6. Joseph Dan, *Hasippur haivri bimei habenayim* (Jerusalem, 1974), 240.

7. André Jolles, quoted in Robert Scholes, *Structuralism in Literature* (New Haven, 1974), 46.

8. David Tamar, "The Ari and Rabbi Hayyim Vital as Messiah Son of Joseph" (in Hebrew), *Sefunot* 7 (1963): 169–177.

9. Gershom Scholem, *On the Kabbalah and Its Symbolism* (New York, 1965), 118–157.

10. Joseph Dan ("Sifrut hashevahim, mizrah, umaarav," *Peamim* 26 [1986]: 80–81) is laying the foundations for a study of the Jewish hagiographical story. He contends that the collections of legends of the Ari serve as a prototype for later collections of biographical legends, including *Shivhei habesht* (1815), the classic collection of legends pertaining to the Baal Shem Tov. He claims, furthermore, that they constitute a behavioral as well as a literary convention in that the type and qualities of holy men in the following centuries come to mirror those of the Ari as portrayed in legend.

11. This introduction, along with some of the explicative and interpretative comments in the notes following the stories, reflects and draws from articles I have written on this subject. These include: "The Dialectic of *Tikkun* in the Legends of the Ari," *Prooftexts* 5 (1985): 33–44; "Hakham and Hasid: The Paradoxical Story in the Kabbalistic Ethical Literature," *Hebrew Studies* 25 (1984): 52–61; and "The Metamorphosis of Narrative Traditions: Two Stories from Sixteenth-Century Safed," *AJS Review* 10 (1985): 165–180. Material from the above articles appears here with permission of the journals.

Sources

Emek hamelekh by Naphtali Bacharach (Amsterdam, 1648), one of the earliest published systematic statements of Lurianic Kabbalah. The series of introductions to this work include several of the Ari legends.

Hemdat yamim, a compendium describing the holy days of the Jewish year, first published in Smyrna, in 1731. All references in this collection refer to the 1763 edition, published in Leghorn and consisting of four volumes: the New Moon (and other occasions), the Sabbath, the Festivals, and the Days of Awe. This work has historically been the subject of polemical debate that extends into current scholarship. The anonymous work represents the moderate mode of Sabbateanism, which remained loyal to rabbinic law and reflects the norms of piety associated with Lurianic Kabbalah. Through his identification of the book's sources, Isaiah Tishby has pinpointed the time of the composition of this anonymous work as being very close to the date of its initial appearance in print.

Kav hayashar by Zvi Hirsch ben Aaron Samuel Kaidanover (Frankfurt, 1705). An example of popular kabbalistic literature, this work makes no attempt at a systematic presentation of kabbalistic ideas but focuses instead on basic ethical values.

Kol sasson by Sasson ben Mordecai Shindookh (Leghorn, 1859; Baghdad, 1891). This book belongs to the kabbalistic ethical writing that flourished in Near Eastern Jewish communities through a later period. The author, a rabbi, poet, and *ḥazzan* in Baghdad (1747–1830), made extensive use of parables in his presentation of basic ethical values.

Midrash talpiot by Rabbi Elijah ha-Kohen the Itamari (Smyrna, 1736). This anthology of sources is arranged according to topics.

Mishnat ḥakhamim by Moses Hagiz (Wandsbeck, 1733). Written by a noted talmudist and vehement opponent of Sabbateanism, this work contains stories not found in other volumes of this literature including a legend of the Ari, "The Former Marrano's Offering."

Naggid umetsaveh by Jacob ben Hayyim Zemah (Amsterdam, 1712). This work presents an account of traditions of the Ari in the realm of moral and religious practices. The story "The Child's Prophecy" appears as an appendix to the second edition of this work published in Constantinople, in 1726.

Or hayashar by Meir Poppers (Amsterdam, 1709). This work, which reflects the teaching of Lurianic Kabbalah, is arranged according to the three pillars of Torah, worship, and acts of loving-kindness with which many stories are interwoven.

Reshit ḥokhmah by Elijah ben Moses de Vidas (Venice, 1579). Written by a student of Rabbi Moses Cordovero, this work is a classic statement of kabbalistic ethics. Widely disseminated, the book was published numerous times and often appeared in abridged form as well.

Seder hayom by Moses ben Makhir (Venice, 1599). Written by the head of a yeshiva in Ein Zeitun, near Safed, this work is a compendium of liturgical and ritual practice. It includes the observances that emerged in Safed and is credited with contributing to the spread and acceptance of those practices much beyond Safed itself.

Sefer ḥaredim by Eliezer Azikri (Venice, 1601), a follower of Rabbi Moses Cordovero. It was composed in connection with the Safed *ḥavurot*, small circles formed for the purpose of study and spiritual living, in which the author was a leading figure. This kabbalistic ethical text also includes within its discourse love poems to God, including the well-known *Yedid nefesh*.

Shulḥan arukh shel haari by Jacob Zemah (Frankfurt an der Oder, 1690). This work, similar in nature and also in content to *Naggid umetsaveh*, appeared about 1660 and includes the account of "Gadiel, the Lad."

The Study of Torah

The Walking Book

The reward of a pious man who, having access to but a single religious text, studied it with great devotion.

Once there was a Hasid living in a small village. He had no books whatsoever except one tractate of the Talmud, Ḥagigah,[1] and all his days he studied that tractate with devotion. He lived a very long life, and at the end, prior to his death, that tractate assumed the form of a woman.[2] Then, following his death, she walked before him, showing him the way to Paradise.[3]

Kav hayashar 14:7

1. Dealing with the special sacrifice offered on the festivals.

2. The female personification of the tractate is appropriate as an object of the Hasid's love; it might also reflect the female gender of the Hebrew word *torah*.

3. The same legend is found also in Jacob Luzzato, *Kaftor vaferaḥ* (Basel, 1581), 71; Isaac Aboab, *Menorat hamaor* (Mantua, 1573), 72; and Moses Gaster, ed., *Maaseh Buch,* vol. 2 (Philadelphia, 1934), 648, no. 247.

A Princess
Locked in a Tower

A parable of what is required of a student in
order to unlock the true meaning of Torah.

There was a princess who was locked within a tower that was completely closed on all sides. She was alone in the house, except for the maidens worthy of serving her. Only by dint of tremendous effort could one find an entrance to the tower, and then one had still to search for the keys capable of opening it. After opening the initial, outer opening, one found chambers within chambers, all of them well locked.

The king had decided against giving his daughter to anyone on the basis of wealth, appearance, family pedigree, or any other criterion of that nature. Rather, he would give her to the one to whom—while attempting to win her love—she would reveal herself from the window to inform him of the location of the opening. Thus he would have to be wise and of sharp mind, seeking key after key in order to enter into the interior chambers of the princess's abode. From that person the king would not withhold his daughter but would give her to him as a wife.

The king announced this challenge throughout his realm, and many came to that tower from the ends of the earth. They encompassed the tower at all hours with all kinds of songs and praises and with various melodies to awaken the heart of the young woman: Perhaps she would find delight in the love of one of them and would reveal herself to him through the holes and cracks. Each suitor afflicted his soul with fasting, both in the heat of the day and in the cold of night, hoping that perhaps she might favor him.

But all those efforts were to no avail because, thinking that in only a brief duration of time one might find the object of his quest, none of them persisted. In truth, one cannot so easily acquire the king's daughter as a wife. In those cases she was not even aware of the suitor's presence, nor did she move from her place. Since those men concluded that they had tried their best without succeeding, they were perplexed and greatly disappointed. They had exhausted themselves to find only dismay.

Then others, hearing of the princess and her beauty and character, came from the islands of the sea and from the ends of the earth and, likewise, encircled the tower from early morning until late at night. They lingered there longer than the first ones had, and they brought with them instruments and composed melodies as well as soothing and flattering utterances to seek the princess's love and to entreat her so that they might not fail. But in the end they too achieved nothing, and they left greatly disappointed.

New candidates arrived daily from east and west hoping to be able to acquire this treasure by touching the young woman's heart so that she might reveal herself to them. They hoped that their words might please her and remained for some time. But, upon seeing that they did not succeed, they too returned home disappointed.

And so people despaired of the quest until one bright lad, exceedingly poor, appeared, thinking: "It is not possible that this tower was built without an opening by which to enter and leave. I will remain for forty days and forty nights if necessary until I find some opening or window through which I'll be able to catch sight of the king's daughter and to speak to her. Then either she will grant my request or I will die because of her." He came with arduous desire, walking back and forth around the tower for days and even years until, at last, he found a windowlike opening in the tower. He began scratching it, and after some dust and pebbles fell from it, he discovered a tiny hole. He then began to shout and scream day after day, calling to the princess in a loud voice and pleading with her that she might favor him.

When she saw that he had already begun to discover the place and had gone to so much trouble and labor to seek her love, the princess's compassion was stirred. She began to speak words of encouragement, telling him not to despair of all his trouble, for his reward would yet come. He rejoiced and was glad, for the one who makes the effort to prepare for the Day of Rest prior to the Sabbath is able to eat on the Sabbath itself.[1] And as he had begun, so he would persist until he found the opening and actually could enter. He made the effort, day after day, until he found such an opening in the wall; he went on to scratch at it until he opened it and entered.

Then he began to call and shout to the princess, begging her to open for him the inner chambers that would bring him into her very quarters, until he actually beheld her with his own eyes. She disclosed to him the place where the keys were located. He took one key and opened one chamber, and with another key he opened another until, little by little, by virtue of his presence of mind and of intelligence, he opened them all, one by one.

And as the princess realized the extent of his desire for her and all the effort that he had expended for her, she sent to inform her father of all that had happened. The king rejoiced in that man who would now be permitted to enjoy the fruit of his deeds. He wanted his daughter to marry that man. The king also revealed other mysteries to him. And he placed in his hands the keys to the tower, that he might close and open them whenever he chose. And he gave his daughter to him as a wife, and the man ascended, assuming higher and higher positions, until he became a viceroy, and he succeeded in his every endeavor . . .

Seder hayom 22a (Slavita, 1793)

1. Avodah Zarah 3a.

A manuscript of Midrash Tanḥuma, which Solomon Buber found at Oxford, includes a legend relating to King Solomon that has many similarities to this parable. In that source, Solomon sought to avoid his daughter's marriage to a lad of extreme poverty, a match foretold by his astrologers. To prevent such a match, the king placed his beautiful daughter in a tall tower situated in the midst of the sea, a tower having no opening other than an inaccessible one on top. But when, one cold evening, that poor lad sought to warm himself by wrapping himself in the corpse of an ox, a large bird proceeded to carry him, together with the dead animal, to that very tower where the princess was concealed. When the guest came to the attention of the king after the couple had already married, having signed a *ketubbah* (marriage document) with blood and having called angels as witnesses, Solomon understood that the poor lad, who was a scribe and was blessed with a sharp mind, was the man of whom the stars had foretold. He reconciled himself to the inevitable, even joyously accepting the match (Midrash Tanḥuma, ed. Solomon Buber [New York, 1946], 136, no. 42).

The figure of a tower in connection with an attempt to avoid the inevitable (Stith Thompson, *Motif-Index of Folk-Literature* [Bloomington, 1955], M. 372: "Confinement in Tower to Avoid Fulfillment of Prophecy") occurs elsewhere in Jewish legends relating to Solomon (Moses Gaster, ed., *The Exempla of the Rabbis* [London-

Leipzig, 1924], 121, no. 336). Islamic legends also relate the biblical king to the same thematics of fate and destiny, even though in those stories Solomon's position on the subject was quite different.

While many elements from the older source are retained in the parable in *Seder hayom,* the nature of the story has been transformed. In addition to the introduction of the motif of the suitor contest (Stith Thompson, *Motif-Index of Folk-Literature* [Bloomington, 1955], H.331), the older legend has been remolded into a parable of the divine. The theme of the futility of seeking to avoid the inevitable is no longer the subject of the story: Significantly, the king in the parable does not seek to avoid giving his daughter to a poor lad. To the contrary, it is emphasized that the king, representing God, invites all interested young men, irrespective of wealth, appearance, or family background, to attempt to enter the tower. All irony has disappeared from the tale.

A catalyst in the transformation of a legend, actually a tale of delight, into a parable of God, the Torah, and the mystic, can be located in another parable, which is found in the Zohar (2:98b–99b): a story describing a palace closed from all sides housing a lovely maiden. The maiden has a lover of whom the world is unaware. As he passes ceaselessly in front of the palace, she makes a tiny opening that only he can see and reveals her face to him, only to disappear from his sight immediately afterward. The Zohar then informs the reader that, like that beautiful woman in the palace who momentarily reveals herself in order to arouse her beloved—while others do not see her at all—so the Torah discloses itself to the one who loves it. It reveals itself gradually, leading its beloved student to ever-deeper levels of understanding, proceeding from the simple meaning of the text to the profounder levels of mystical interpretation. In the parable found in *Seder hayom,* the image of the closed tower, recalling the older midrashic legend, acquired new significance drawn from the zoharic image of the closed palace.

Seder hayom, written by Moses ben Makhir, who headed an academy in Ein Zeitun in the vicinity of Safed, became a popular commentary and guide to Jewish liturgy and ritual. The author included this parable in the context of his discussion of the importance of studying Torah prior to leaving the house of prayer in the morning. Learning, he stresses, requires persistence, regularity, and attentiveness even to the most minute details (Stith Thompson, *Motif-Index of Folk-Literature* [Bloomington, 1955], Q. 82: "Reward for Perseverance"). Like the suitor who found a very small hole in the tower only after considerable effort, truth does not glare in the student's face but, rather, is found only through attention to the small holes and cracks in the tower, the seemingly insignificant details that may serve as keys by which to understand the real nature of one's subject of study. Ben Makhir states that when God beholds one's persistence and the strength of one's desire to understand, He then discloses the truth to that person. Superficial study will never lead the student beyond the literal meaning of the text—the essence of the Torah, Ben Makhir accentuates, is necessarily hidden from the eyes of each and every student at the outset of his studies.

The claim that the fullness of the Torah's truth lies far beneath the surface is borrowed from the medieval philosophical tradition (note Maimonides, *Guide of the Perplexed* 1:33, 2:48; also the introduction to Saadiah, *Emunot vedeot*) and applied to the mystic tradition of Kabbalah, which is equated with the deeper meaning of the Torah. In contrast to the zoharic parable, the emphatic point in the parable and its interpretation in both *Seder hayom* and *Ḥemdat yamim* (1763) *Moadim* 51ab is not the Torah's disclosure but, rather, the need for patient effort and labor on the part of the student. Both, it is stressed, are necessary. The Torah's insights transcend what the mind, by its own powers, is capable of attaining. Insight into the Torah is an act of revelation, and such revelation is the Torah's response to the true seeker.

The parable portrays the paradox of a mystic approach to the Torah: The truth of the Torah is concealed, heavily guarded within a labyrinth of chambers within chambers, each requiring special keys. Yet, at the same time, it is God's intent both that human beings make the effort to discover that hidden truth and, furthermore, that they succeed in the endeavor. The truth of Torah is hidden not in order to bar them from it but rather to present the kind of challenge necessary to enable a person to penetrate to the depth of that truth. Similarly, the mystic, experiencing the Torah as an enigma beyond his grasp, is yet confident that, like the locked tower, it too must have a key.

When this parable is compared with the zoharic parable of the palace, one crucial difference emerges. The zoharic parable speaks of the one lover whom the Torah leads to more and more inner dimensions of its meaning, a lover hidden from the notice of human society; the very fact of the princess's presence in the palace is a guarded secret. The parable found in the two later sources, by contrast, suggests that God chooses to encourage as many as possible to seek the way to mystic truth. Throughout his vast realm, the king announces his daughter's presence in the tower in order to summon to the test all those who wish to accept the challenge to seek her.

In the light of this contrast, the later parable can be seen to mirror the transition from the conception of Kabbalah as an esoteric teaching designated only for the spiritual elite—a teaching to be zealously hidden and guarded—to a much more popular conception of mystic learning as a teaching intended for the many. Such a transition was very characteristic of the world of sixteenth-century Jewish mystical thought.

The Seven Guests
in True Togetherness

*The appearance of seven heavenly guests together
in a* sukkah *testifies to the awesome quality of
Torah study on the part of a teacher and his
student.*

Once a wondrous rabbi was sitting and studying in his *sukkah* together
with his student. While the two were still studying, the student began
to tremble. He rose, ran out, and came back; and in his hand was a
live coal and a pair of tongs.[1] His master was astonished at this sight
for he perceived the pupil putting the live coal into the hand of another,
unseen, within the *sukkah* and kindling something.

The rabbi said to him, "What is this, my son? Why do you stand
shaking and trembling and doing these things?" He feared that perhaps
a spirit of foolishness or the madness of depression, God forbid, had
seized him.

But the student answered him, "Does not my master see all these
elders among us?" And he counted them, "One, two, three, four, five,
six, seven. And because it is said, 'In every place incense is burnt and
offered to My Name,'[2] they requested of me to bring a live coal to
exemplify the incense that is brought into being through our act of
Torah study." The student also gave signs of the order of their places,
indicating where each was seated: Abraham in the south, Isaac in the
north, and Jacob in the east; and with Abraham in the south sat Moses,
our teacher—may he rest in peace—and Aaron sat with Isaac in the
north, while Joseph and David[3] were situated along the western side
of the *sukkah*.

The rabbi, hearing the words of his student, was utterly amazed
at the scene, and he saw that the power of the student exceeded that
of the master. For the former was able to see all that the sages of the
Zohar had revealed to us concerning the seven heavenly guests who
come with the illumination of their soul-sparks to all the *sukkot* of Israel.
And because the rabbi and the student were sitting together and studying Torah with awe and dread, all those sparks gathered together there,
and the eye was able to perceive them face-to-face. Blessed is the eye
that has seen all of them.[4]

And ever since that time, the rabbi and the student stood in dread and awe, studying Torah all the days of the festival until hardly a word of everyday conversation was heard within their *sukkah*. From then on, that saintly man became an eminent guardian of this mitzvah: to warn all the people against careless and light-headed behavior while in their *sukkot* in the presence of the saintly ones, and against all similar things of that nature.

Ḥemdat yamim, Moadim 73a

1. Isaiah 6:6.
2. Malachi 1:11.
3. The *ushpizin*, the seven heavenly guests who are said to visit the *sukkah*, each on his own particular evening of the Sukkot festival, are Abraham, Isaac, Jacob, Moses, Aaron, Joseph, and David. The practice of welcoming the *ushpizin* began, it appears, in the days of the Ari, though the concept is based upon a statement in the Zohar (3:103b–104a) explaining that the portions of the seven heavenly guests are to be given to the poor. According to Kabbalistic lore, the seven guests represent the seven lower spheres of the Godhead, and dwelling in the *sukkah* constitutes a contact with those seven spheres (See Isaiah Tishby, *Mishnat hazohar*, vol. 2 [Jerusalem, 1961] 521).
4. An allusion to the piyyut, *ashre ayin raata zot* ("Blessed is the eye which has seen this"). This expression is from the Avodah of the Yom Kippur liturgy, where it refers to the sight of the High Priest emerging from the Holy of Holies on that day.

On the surface, the opening of the tale extols the act of studying together in the *sukkah* in a pronounced mood of reverence. While according to a tradition found in the Zohar (3:103b–104a), each of the seven biblical personages normally visits the *sukkah* on one evening of the Sukkot festival, the act of study by this particular teacher and his student in such true togetherness and in such a truly awesome mood brought about the coming together of all the *ushpizin* at one time.

At the beginning, the reader hears of the wondrous rabbi, while, further into the story, the rabbi errs in his judgment of what he sees in his pupil's behavior. It is true that their act of togetherness in study invoked the visible presence of the soul-sparks of all seven *ushpizin*—but only to the student; they are not visible to the teacher. The expectations of the reader, or listener, are reversed: The student, it turns out, is on a higher level than his master, who perceives the wondrous occurrence only on the authority of the student's words. A story such as this could grow in the soil of the motif of the *yenuka*—the wise, often wondrously wise, child or pupil—and is found, in particular, in the Zohar and in the literature it inspired (see "Gadiel, the Lad" in this volume).

The story emphasizes not simply the study of Torah but the mood of awe and trembling that characterizes it, pointing to a metaintellectual value. Similarly, if Torah knowledge itself constituted the value center of the tale, the teacher, with his presumably greater knowledge would be the exemplary figure in the narrative. The pupil, however, possesses spiritual power far surpassing that of his teacher, and his power is not equivalent to or dependent upon the kind of knowledge that can be taught. His knowledge and his power are, rather, mystic in character.

The ideal of the Hasid, inherited from earlier medieval pietistic literature, has merged with that of the mystic. Hence the tale of two Jews studying together so earnestly operates on a more profound level as a tale of a learned sage and a mystic-pietist, a person of deep inner spiritual experience.

Gadiel, the Lad

A youth who had died a martyr's death for his
devotion to the study of Torah teaches in a
heavenly academy hidden in the celestial worlds.

In the chamber of brightness[1] in the celestial Garden of Eden there is
a master of an academy who is hidden and concealed in the chamber
of the bird's nest.[2] He is Rabbi Gadiel, the lad, who reveals all the
depths of the Torah and its hidden things; and the longing of all the
saintly is directed toward him.

Rabbi Gadiel was born in the days of the forced apostasy,[3] and he
learned Torah in a cave. When he was seven years old gentiles came
and found him studying, and they cut his body into pieces. But his
soul ascended on high, and it is said that the sight of brightness around
him is like that of the rainbow[4] on a rainy day, and as the view of the
likeness of God's Glory. The Holy One, blessed be He, placed him in
His presence, and He swore to grant him the chamber of brightness
and to reveal through him, there in the Garden of Eden, those mysteries
of Torah that were not previously disclosed.

All the righteous who are in the Garden of Eden desire to see him,
and they hear from him the deep and hidden things of the Torah.
When he pronounces the letters of the Ineffable Name of God, the
letters become manifest and glisten over his head, and all the righteous
rejoice in him. He, however, falls upon his face, wailing and weeping
because he did not merit having a son in this world.[5] Joshua the son
of Jehotsedek[6] the High Priest stands and consoles him, taking hold
of him, raising him up on his feet, and saying, "Rise up, for hundreds
upon hundreds[7] are your sons."

Rabbi Johanan ben Zakkai[8] fasted seventy times to see him and in
a dream was shown the hidden things of the seven firmaments. And
following them he saw him in the very highest firmament, shining like
the light of the firmament with seventy angels encompassing him, and
fifty keys in his hand, and groups of the righteous before him, and the
letters of the Ineffable Name glistening upon his head. But then he
was immediately hidden and could not be seen. Rabbi Johanan ben
Zakkai was told, "Up to this point you are permitted," and the appearance was like that of the rainbow.[9]

Sages looked into the matter of the father who merited such a son.
They found that the man never gazed at the countenance of a wicked

person,[10] never looked at the bow of the sign of the covenant,[11] never extended his hand beneath his navel, and never paused in his study for worldly pursuits. There was not a saintly person in the world in whose distress he did not feel sorrow, and he never spoke idle words but, rather, occupied himself with Torah and its mitzvot.[12] He died immediately after he begat a son such as this, and the mother too died immediately after giving birth to him. Gadiel remained an orphan and grew up in great sorrow and poverty. He studied much Torah and was killed for the Sanctification of God's Name.[13] All this he merited.

Shulḥan arukh shel haari 27d–28b

1. *Noga,* the lowest of the celestial firmaments in the Kabbalistic world picture.

2. A hidden chamber of the celestial Eden where, according to the Zohar (2:8a), the Messiah resides. A thousand palaces of longing are concealed there. Only the Messiah may enter into the chamber where he weeps for the plight of Israel in exile. Gershom Scholem ("Mekorotav shel 'maase rabi gadiel hatinok' besifrut hakabbalah," in *Leagnon Shai,* ed. Dov Sadan and Efraim E. Urbach [Jerusalem, 1959], 296) explained the name in terms of the rabbinic midrash (Deuteronomy Rabba 6 on Deuteronomy 22:6–7) that suggests, on the basis of midrashic word association, that the Messiah's coming will be hastened through the merit of fulfilling the command to send away the mother bird from the nest before taking her young.

3. During the reign of the Roman Emperor Hadrian, in the first half of the second century C.E.

4. In the version of the tale included in *Seder gan eden* (Adolf Jellinek, ed., *Bet hamidrash,* vol. 3 [Jerusalem, 1938], 136–137; Judah D. Eisenstein, *Otsar midrashim,* vol. 1 [New York, 1915], 87; and also in *Tsavat rabi eliezer hagadol, Orḥot ḥayyim* [Prague, 1612]), Gadiel's soul, upon being brought up to Paradise, proclaimed in words taken from Ezekiel 1:28: "As the appearance of the rainbow on a rainy day is the appearance of brightness all around; it is the sight of the image of the Lord's Glory."

5. According to *Tsavat rabi eliezer hagadol,* fols. 8b–9a.

6. Mentioned in Zechariah 3:2. According to the Jerusalem Talmud Taanit 4, 69b, he was the only young priest who escaped death at the time of the destruction of Jerusalem by the Babylonians. According to Babylonian Talmud Sanhedrin 93a, he was one of the three persons whom Nebuchadnezzar cast into the fiery furnace.

7. Rashi on Sanhedrin 98a.

8. Leader of the Pharisees at the time of the destruction of the Second Commonwealth in 70 C.E. and a leading figure in the emergence of rabbinic Judaism.

9. According to the Zohar 1:71a, the color of the rainbow mirrors precisely the supernal vision. While now its colors are dull in comparison, with redemption the rainbow will again have resplendent colors that will give light to the world. Also Zohar 3:84a. Gazing at a rainbow is considered equivalent to gazing at the Divine Presence (Zohar 3:66b).

10. Megillah 28a, where, in the name of Rabbi Johanan, it is forbidden to do so.

In one passage the Zohar (3:84a) forbids looking upon the rainbow and upon the place of circumcision. Both, in different ways, reflect or signify the divine.

11. The phallus, according to *Tsaavat rabi eliezer hagadol*, fol. 9a. In the text of *Ḥemdat yamim*, *Shabbat* 65a, it could be understood either as the rainbow (Ḥagigah 16a forbids looking at the rainbow because it symbolizes the Divine Glory; Zohar 3:66b speaks of a brilliant rainbow that appeared with the splitting of the Red Sea, so that gazing at the rainbow is, in a sense, gazing at the Divine Presence) or as the phallus, a meaning that fits its textual context. In Sota 36b, and similarly in *Genesis Rabba* 98:20, the term is understood to signify male sexual passion.

12. Righteous and pious deeds.

13. Traditional term for martyrdom.

Gershom Scholem suggests that the figure of Gadiel was originally a merging of the angel Gadiel, mentioned in the Zohar, and Metatron, similarly a lad who instructed children as well as keeper of the celestial keys. In tracing the development of the Gadiel legend, Scholem ("Mekorotav shel 'maase rabi gadiel hatinok' ") who identifies it as part of the literature of the Zohar, remarks that the state of mind of the Kabbalists is mirrored in the legend in which the one who merits proximity to the Messiah is not a renowned scholar but, rather, a child genius of complete purity of soul. It is interesting that in the source in *Orḥot ḥayyim* (probably thirteenth century), the sixth firmament of the celestial paradise is inhabited by young schoolchildren who never sinned, and each midnight they go up to the higher academy where God Himself instructs them in Torah.

Among the threads running through the account is the motif of hiddenness, which is accentuated by Gadiel's concealed state in his celestial chamber. During his brief life, as a parallel, he hid in a cave; in Paradise, the hidden things of the Torah are revealed through him. There he remains hidden from human eyes, and even though Rabbi Johanan ben Zakkai succeeded in beholding him, that revelation was of only momentary duration.

The text of the legend is built also upon the polarity of the depths and the heights. The image of the cave is connected with the generation of scholars who went into hiding during the time of the Hadrianic decrees that prohibited the study and teaching of Torah. The cave, hidden below the ground, contrasts with the upper worlds. Because of Gadiel's unlimited devotion to study in a cave and his torturous death there, his soul ascends to its place in Paradise where he is able to know and reveal the *deep* secrets of the Torah. Whereas a cave is a place of darkness, Gadiel and his chamber in Paradise are characterized by unbounded brightness.

Yet, despite that brightness and celestial stature, Gadiel sorrows that, unlike his father, he did not have the chance to beget a son in holiness. This jarring element in the narrative, which originated in Christian Spain, may perhaps express a polemical note against the ascetic requirements of the Christian priesthood: The fathering of a child is seen as a legitimate human and spiritual longing, and the lack of a child is not compensated even by all the blessings of a celestial existence.

The innocence of the child-student is mirrored in his father's sexual morality, which, in part, merited his having such a son. It also is mirrored in his being the object of the desire and longing of the righteous and pious. The word *taavah* (desire) can indicate sexual longing, a kind of desire here transmuted into the longing for holiness represented in the strong desire to behold Gadiel, who longs to have fathered a son.

The Failing of Torah without Prayer

*A devoted student is punished because, despite
warning, he ignored the need to pray.*

Nahmanides[1] had a student who sought Torah with such wondrous
longing and desire that he would not allow himself to sleep. And if he
ate in order to sustain his body, even then the book was open before
him, his eyes always focused upon the pages. But he would not pray,
due to his intense love for studying Torah.

Nahmanides—may his memory be for a blessing—would constantly warn him and tell him: "Eat at mealtime, and sleep when it is
time to sleep, and offer your prayer when it is time to pray, and the
merit of the Torah will then be with you and will guard you and keep
you in life. But should you transgress by overlooking prayer, then it
will avenge its insult before the Holy One, blessed be He, and you will
consequently be punished, Heaven forbid! So take heed concerning
prayer."

But the student neither paid attention to his teacher's words nor
took them to heart. Only a few days later, when the student had gone
to the marketplace to purchase something, he returned home to find a
knight lying with his virgin daughter, raping her upon the very table
at which he had always studied. And he lamented her fate many days.

His teacher, Nahmanides, asked him: "Did I not warn you to be
careful concerning the order of prayer that the sages instituted? For
each day a person must pray, 'May it be Your will, Lord, our God,
and God of our fathers, to save us this day from an evil person, and
so forth.[2] But you did not listen to me, and therefore this distress has
befallen your daughter."

And from that time on, the student recognized that Divine Provi-
dence accounted for the punishment he had received for his failure to
pray, and he began to pray properly.

Kav hayashar 8:7–8

---

1. Moses ben Nahman (*Ramban*) (1195–1270), a noted scholar and biblical
exegete of the Spanish period.
2. Words taken from the introductory passages of the morning liturgy.

This account is told in the name of Isaiah Hasid with the claim that he had heard it, in turn, from Judah the Hasid. It is quoted from the seventeenth-century work by Abraham ben Isaac Hayyuth, *Sefer holekh tamim* (Cracow, 1634), no. 435. The latter, in turn, quotes the story from *Sefer meirat enayim* ([Jerusalem, 1975], 78, based on MS Parma 77, *Vayishlah*) by Rabbi Isaac ben Samuel (*Rivash*) of Acre, a Kabbalist of the late thirteenth and early fourteenth centuries. In that work the story is included in a bitter polemic against philosophy and its negative impact upon religious life and observance. In certain extant and unabridged manuscripts of *Sefer meirat enayim* (N. 1619, N. 1621, N. 1623, all located at the Bodleian Library, Oxford) the legend speaks of a student of Maimonides, not Nahmanides, presumably a scribal error. In both *Kav hayashar* and *Hemdat yamim* (1763), *Yamim noraim* 14b, the story is completely divorced from its earlier context of antiphilosophical polemic.

The story opens with a summary of the pupil's daily routine and then reports his master's repeated warnings. In the Hebrew, both employ the word *tamid* (always), signifying an extended period of time. Once decreed, however, the punishment comes swiftly.

One would expect the student's refraining from sleep to evoke admiration in a milieu that esteemed the ascetic practice of awakening in the middle of the night to engage in prayer and study—thereby conquering the body's desire for sleep. Therefore the student's refusal to take time from his study in order to pray seems to constitute the one flaw in one who is otherwise, on the surface of things, a deeply dedicated student.

His teacher, however, mandates from him three activities—eating, sleeping, and prayer—all of which would compete timewise with Torah study. Furthermore he warns him that prayer, if neglected, will bring its complaint directly before God (Stith Thompson, *Motif-Index of Folk-Literature* [Bloomington, 1955], Q. 233.1: "Neglect to Pray Punished"). Both prayer and God will then stand in opposition to the student, an utter denial of his assumption that God approves of his one-sided devotion to Torah study at the expense of prayer.

The story is constructed according to a pattern consisting of a warning, disregard of the warning, the tragic punishment, the student's belated recognition of his wrongdoing, and his consequent change of behavior. In this case, however, the change occurs too late to avert punishment. Although his teacher had admonished him to take time to pray, the full gravity of the sin is not apparent from the admonition. That is revealed only in the dreadful punishment that follows, a punishment that explicitly conveys the harsh judgment of the sin of engaging in such study without prayer: The knight rapes the daughter on the very table at which her father has always studied. In the spirit of the principle of "measure for measure," the knight's abominable act mirrors the divine evaluation of the student's learning when not accompanied by prayer. The student's "wondrous desire" for Torah is reduced to the level of the knight's immoral desire for the daughter.

While advocating the importance of Torah study as a basic component of the traditional complex of Jewish values, the popular pietistic writings also convey an unambiguous distrust of study of Torah that is not accompanied by piety.

Deeds of Compassion
and Responsibility

The Unseen Guest

A student who acted compassionately, in the spirit
of a long-deceased sage, is accompanied by the
famous sage's presence.

One time our teacher and rabbi, Samuel de Uceda, author of *Sefer midrash shemuel,*[1] came to the Ari, and the latter rose to his full height and greeted him, taking him by the hand and seating him at his right side. Rabbi Samuel told him what he needed to relate to him and left. After he had gone, Rabbi Hayyim Vital—may his memory be for a blessing—asked the Ari, "Why did my teacher rise in the presence of this young man and honor him as he did?" And the Ari said, "I rose before the presence of Rabbi Phinehas ben Jair,[2] who entered together with him above his head, and he did this because Samuel did one mitzvah that Rabbi Phinehas ben Jair used to fulfill; therefore the sage's soul clad itself in Rabbi Samuel so that it might help him in similar mitzvot. And this is the secret, "God helps him who seeks to improve."[3]

Upon hearing this, Rabbi Hayyim immediately ran after Rabbi Samuel to ask him what mitzvah he had done that very day. As he caught up with him he asked, "Please, tell me what is the mitzvah that you fulfilled this day?" And he explained what the Ari had related to them.

Rabbi Samuel told him, "Today, before dawn,[4] as I was on my way to be one of the first ten to arrive in the house of prayer, I passed a house from which I heard much weeping. When I entered to inquire why there was crying, I saw them all naked, for thieves had entered during the night and had taken everything they possessed. Out of compassion for them, I removed my outer garment and gave it to them, and I went home to put on my Sabbath garment."

When Rabbi Hayyim returned to the Ari, the latter told him, "Certainly because of this mitzvah in which Rabbi Samuel clothed the naked, the soul of Rabbi Phinehas ben Jair clad itself in him, for Rabbi Phinehas also used to relate to all people with compassion all the days of his life."

Emek hamelekh, Introduction, 11a

1. A commentary on Mishna Avot published in Venice in 1579.
2. A second-century sage and son-in-law of Rabbi Simeon bar Yohai. He is

remembered for his saintliness, which is described in legendary terms. In the Zohar, where he is identified as the father-in-law of Rabbi Simeon bar Yohai, Phinehas ben Jair, though deceased, continues at times to appear to his son-in-law (Zohar, Idra Zutra). Our legend is thus seen to be based on the earlier, zoharic tradition.

3. "God assists him who comes to purify himself." (Shabbat 104a).

4. "The morning watch," last third of the night.

The Wind
and the Locusts

*A plague of locusts threatens, signaling the
suffering of a man bereft of his means of
livelihood. When help is extended to him, the
threat departs.*

The Ari—may he rest in peace—was once sitting with his students in
the very field where the prophet Hosea, son of Beeri, was buried. And
while the Ari was expounding the hidden meanings of the Torah—in
the midst of his lecture—he suddenly exclaimed, "For God's sake, hurry
and contribute alms, and let us send them to help a poor man named
Jacob Alterutz who resides nearby. For he is sitting and weeping and
complaining bitterly to God concerning his poverty. And his voice is
ascending upward, cleaving all the firmaments and entering before the
very presence of the Holy One, blessed be He, who feels wrath toward
the entire town because of this poor man for whom none has shown
compassion. Just now I hear an announcement resounding throughout
all the firmaments, a decree of angels ordering a heavy plague of locusts
to arrive throughout the area surrounding Safed to consume all the
gathered grain and the standing corn and even the olive trees and grape
vines. So hurry and send him alms; perhaps, with God's help, we shall
be able to annul the decree."

Immediately everyone present willingly contributed, and the Ari
turned the money over to his student, Rabbi Isaac ha-Kohen, ordering
him to hurry to Jacob Alterutz's home and give the money to him.
Quickly Rabbi Isaac ha-Kohen ran to the house of Jacob Alterutz only
to find him at the entrance of his home, weeping in supplication. When
the student asked, "Sir, why are you crying?" Jacob Alterutz explained
that his water jug had broken to pieces and, penniless and unable to
acquire another in its place, he did not know what to do in the face
of his cruel distress and poverty. Rabbi Isaac ha-Kohen immediately
handed him the money and blessed him, experiencing true joy.

When Rabbi Isaac returned, his teacher, the Ari, announced that
the decree had been annulled, that there was now nothing to fear.
While they were yet speaking, a strong wind began to blow, bearing
locusts beyond number, and the students were struck by terror. But

the Ari reassured them, "Have no fear, for the decree is already annulled."

And so it was that the locusts all flew in the direction of the Mediterranean and drowned there in the water without a single one remaining in all the land.[1]

Kav hayashar 9:7–9

1. The legend is found also in *Shivḥe haari* (Meir Benayahu [Jerusalem 1967], 171); in Joseph Solomon Delmedigo, *Sefer taalumot ḥokhmah* (Basel, 1629), 39a; and in *Emek hamelekh* (Amsterdam, 1648), Introduction, 12a. The Ari's ability to ascertain the burial site of the biblical prophet prepares the reader to accept the sage's wondrous knowledge as exemplified in the rest of the story. The legend illustrates the social consciousness that characterized the pietism of sixteenth-century Safed and also echoes the biblical association of plagues and locusts in the account of the Exodus from Egypt.

The Ladder Restored

A woman has become infertile because she
unknowingly caused distress to young chicks.
When the cause of that distress is made known
and corrected, she is able, once again, to bear
children.

... The Ari was once the guest of an important man, a person of integrity who greatly honored his visitor. Prior to his departure, the holy Ari asked his host how he could repay him for his sincere hospitality and for all his efforts on his behalf. The host responded by telling his guest that after having given birth to children his wife became barren; he thought that perhaps the Ari could suggest a remedy to restore his wife's fertility.

The Ari—may he rest in peace—explained that the turning point in her condition had come in connection with another change, "For, you know, standing in your house there used to be a small ladder that the young chicks would use to go up and down to drink water from a pan next to the ladder. They would drink and quench their thirst. Then your wife told the servant girl to remove the ladder. Now, although it was not her intent to cause the chicks distress but simply to make for a clean house, ever since the ladder was removed the chicks have been in distress. Being too young to fly, they suffer from great thirst, and their chirping made its way to the Holy One, blessed be He, who has compassion for all His creatures.[1] It is for this that her state of barrenness has been decreed."

The host returned the ladder to its former place, and the Lord allowed the man's wife to conceive and resume bearing children as before.

Kav hayashar 7:20–21

1. Psalms 145:9.

Compassion is required not only in one's dealings with human needs but also in those related to animals. The Ari's wondrous knowledge, the motif of sin committed even unwittingly when one is not at all aware of one's deeds or of their consequences, and the need to be compassionate to all living things combine to form this legend. The association of birth with compassion for living things and of barrenness as resulting from lack of such compassion is the basis of Agnon's short story, "Kippurim," in *Kol sipurav shel shmuel yosef agnon,* vol. 2 (Jerusalem, 1966), 199–209.

Elijah and the Overlooked Poor Man

In distributing alms, a rabbi overlooked an anonymous poor man. Elijah comes to help the needy, pious man, and a frightening dream warns the rabbi concerning his oversight.

From the elders in Jerusalem I heard of something that had occurred there many years ago. It was the custom in that city for the rabbi to assign and distribute funds for each needy person before the Passover festival.[1] He would similarly distribute the alms fund to those who were poor, humble, and learned.

In those days there was in Jerusalem a man who was pious and wise, exceedingly unassuming, living in a pressing state of poverty. While distributing the funds, the rabbi overlooked that person. And when the days of Nisan[2] arrived with the festival approaching, the man found himself completely without means. All his sons and daughters asked him, "Is there nothing you can do? Look, the Lord's festival is fast approaching. It is already time to burn and remove the *hamets*,[3] and we shall perish before your very eyes because we will not transgress and eat *hamets* during Passover." And while they were speaking in this vein, the water in his pails was depleted, and he cried out because of his poverty and distress.

As he pleaded so fervently in prayer, his cry made its way to God. The Lord gave heed to his cry and felt anger toward the city to the point of wanting to destroy it because of the cry of that devout poor man, clad in hunger and with none to comfort him, until Elijah stood in prayer before Him to turn His wrath away from destruction. Elijah said, "Lord, Lord, compassionate God,[4] do not destroy Your people and Your inheritance. I will, indeed, go down there and look after that poor man to deliver him with honor, for people have forgotten him not in a spirit of transgression or selfish intent but, rather, as a consequence of his extreme meekness."

When that devout poor man rose from his knees and went out into the city streets, Elijah—may his memory be for a blessing—appeared and greeted him. The man returned the greeting and asked him, "What is it that you want?" Elijah replied, "No one has invited me to his home for the festival; and if it pleases you, do me the honor of inviting me to your house for this Passover, and I will reward you." And the pious poor man responded, "Come, praised be God, just as you have said, and stay with me as long as you want; simply tell me your name that we might fulfill your request and honor you." Elijah answered, "This is my name, Rabbi Nissim[5] the Egyptian; and take this money to slaughter and prepare an animal for the meal." The poor devout man took the money and returned home in great joy, telling his wife all that had occurred. And he commanded his household concerning the honor due to the guest, for "he is an old man and a person of importance, and his appearance is like that of an angel of God. So be careful to treat him with respect."

On the day preceding the Passover the pious man said, "I will go out and locate our guest and invite him to come to us," and he encompassed the entire town walking through streets and marketplaces and inquiring of people, "Do you know our guest, Rabbi Nissim the Egyptian, or have you seen him?" And all would respond, "We neither know him, nor have we even heard his name until this moment."

He proceeded to search throughout all the city without finding him until the pious man realized what was obvious: that this man was no ordinary human being but was Elijah—may his memory be for a blessing—who had referred to himself as Rabbi Nissim the Egyptian because of the miracle [*nes*] allowing me to acquire what I need in order to observe properly the Passover festival, which, in turn, is celebrated because of the miracle of Israel in Egypt. And from what remained of that money, the pious man never again lacked sustenance all the rest of his days.[6]

On the first night of the Passover festival, a man whose appearance resembled that of an angel of God appeared in a dream vision to the rabbi of the city of Jerusalem, who was terrified for the man appeared to strangle him while shouting, "How did you do such a thing and forget that poor pious man? Know that you were all close to death, for God, in His wrath, would have brought destruction were it not for Elijah, who pleaded before Him to turn His anger away from destruction and who turned compassionately to the poor one and helped him."

In the morning the rabbi, deeply agitated, sent for that poor man and begged his forgiveness so that he might not die as a consequence of that iniquity. Ever since, the rabbi made it his responsibility to seek out diligently every unassuming poor person or beggar and to assist him.

Ḥemdat yamim, Moadim 10ab

1. The giving of *maot ḥittin* (wheat money) to the needy for Passover is found already in the Jerusalem Talmud *Bava Batra* 1:6, 12d. The practice is codified in Moses Isserles' commentary to *Oraḥ ḥayyim* 429:1.
2. The spring month on the full moon of which the Passover (*pesaḥ*) festival begins.
3. Leaven (food not permissible during Passover).
4. Exodus 34:6.
5. "Miracles."
6. Stith Thompson, *Motif-Index of Folk-Literature* (Bloomington, 1955), Q. 111.2: "Riches as reward [for hospitality]."

Two familiar narrative patterns common in Jewish folktales are present in this story: (1) that iniquity, and in particular miserliness in matters of almsgiving, brings in its wake either punishment or often the threat of punishment, which then leads the sinner to repent with the result that the punishment is averted; and (2) that Elijah continues to save people from situations of distress. In this story the two motifs are interwoven to create a more complex tale.

Elijah came down to Jerusalem with two purposes in mind: to save the poor man and his family from hunger and to save the city from destruction. The nature of Elijah's role in the story mirrors the situation of Abraham in Genesis 18. As God is about to destroy the wicked Cities of the Plain, the patriarch pleads and argues with Him to avert the punishment; like Abraham so Elijah argues against the decree. The tale thus sets up a polarity between the divine judgment and the activity of Elijah. The judgment of God—the quality of justice—is founded upon the logic that a city in which there is no one to comfort the poor does not deserve God's compassion. Yet it is the quality of compassion, represented by Elijah, that ultimately triumphs.

The prayer of the poor man aroused divine judgment: God's intent to destroy the city. But at the very same time that the poor man was praying Elijah also prayed, and his prayer evoked God's compassion for the city and its inhabitants. The two prayers serve opposite ends and lead to results that run counter to one another. The prayer of Elijah annuls the decree of destruction, which was the unintended fruit of the poor man's prayer, while the deed of Elijah annuls the hunger that gave rise to the poor man's prayer itself.

The end of the tale offers the paradox of the Jerusalem rabbi begging forgiveness of the poor man in order that he, the rabbi, might not die as punishment for his disastrous oversight; that is, hierarchical societal norms regarding roles and status are reversed. The life and death of the known and respected rabbi of the city lies in the hands of one who is poor and actually unnoticed in his society. As in the story "Father Abraham Visits a *Sukkah*," this mirror image of accepted norms is disclosed in a dream.

In this kind of moral tale, the polarities of good and evil are typically quite clearly marked. The tale might center around a wicked—or miserly—person who changes his behavior pattern following a threat of severe punishment. Our tale, however, exemplifies a basic deviation from that more conventional pattern: It tells not of a wicked person, nor even of a man basically indifferent to human needs but, rather, of a Jew who is active precisely in the realm of almsgiving. A full thirty days prior to the festival the rabbi had begun distributing funds to the needy. Moreover, as Elijah claims in his pleading before God on behalf of the townspeople, the poor man was forgotten because he had made it so difficult for them to take note of him. Yet, even a deed or misdeed done unwittingly can evoke the gravest consequences: The rabbi had failed to make the additional effort necessary to identify the anonymous needy cases.

The rabbi's failure in this regard is the mirror image of the poor man's quest for his guest in order to bring him home for the Passover festival. The tale describes his searchings with words that recall Song of Songs 3:2, words that suggest, by association, the love with which the poor man sought to locate his guest.

Within the larger context of *Ḥemdat yamim*, the search for the poor and needy in this tale is echoed in the search for *ḥamets*, the removal and burning of all particles of food not fit for use during the Passover festival (17ab), described in the following chapter of the book. The element of search thus reverberates, as it were, both within this tale and from one chapter to the next in the account of preparations for Passover in *Ḥemdat yamim*.

Father Abraham
Visits a Sukkah

A poor beggar, invited with sincerity and gladness to visit a sukkah, proves to be the patriarch Abraham in disguise.

While a Hasid was seated at the table at a gathering with some well-known sages, there appeared a poor man going from door to door begging for a piece of bread. The Hasid immediately rose from his seat to take the poor man's hand and, with great joy, seated him in his own place and served him. He explained, "I am rejoicing today with you because the Lord has brought it about that I am privileged to feed you, here in my *sukkah,*[1] the portion designated for our father, Abraham."[2]

That night the Hasid dreamed that he was drowning in the midst of the sea, and that same poor man came and stretched out his hand to him and delivered him from the deep waters to safety. The Hasid immediately stood to embrace and kiss the poor man and said, "Blessed are you of the Lord; who are you who has saved my life from death? For, unable to withstand the waves, I was but a step away from death by drowning in the deep mire; I came into the depths of the waters and the flood overwhelmed me."[3]

And the man answered the Hasid, "I am Abraham, your father, who came today to your *sukkah* in the guise of that poor man. Blessed are you; how good is your portion, and how pleasant is your lot[4] with all the righteous, and know that no evil decree will befall your household; rather, you shall always enjoy tranquility and shall not know fear of any evil.

The Hasid awoke from his sleep with a joyous heart and a glad soul, for the Lord had granted him these things. And it became his practice each year, all the days of the festival, to prepare, to the full extent of his ability, a special feast for the poor as his gift to them. The Hasid, who became a very learned and pious man, never lacked food even in his advanced years.

From this we can learn the importance of the mitzvah of giving food to the poor during Sukkot even over and above its significance on the other days of the year. For man beholds the outward appearance of things[5] and perceives such people merely as they seem, while in truth they are the image and likeness of the righteous and holy ones of the world who, during the seven days of this holy festival, awaken from their places and are found in the homes and booths of Israel.

Ḥemdat yamim, Moadim 72a

1. A thatched booth constructed as a temporary dwelling for the seven days of the Sukkot festival.
2. See "The Seven Guests in True Togetherness," n. 3. If during the Sukkot festival, the portion of the biblical guest of any particular day is given to the poor, it follows that one must welcome a poor guest on the first evening of the festival *as if* that guest were the patriarch Abraham. The tale takes that formula one step further and erases the simile: The poor guest who appears on the first evening of Sukkot is, indeed, Abraham himself.
3. Psalms 69:3.
4. The words are taken from the introductory section of the morning liturgy.
5. 1 Samuel 16:7.

The pattern and motif of this story recall an earlier story found in the Zohar (2:61a) and included also in Meir Poppers' *Or hayashar, Amud gemilut ḥasadim* 2. One can reasonably assume that the zoharic story, certainly known to the author and to those in his circle, is an obvious source for the narrative found in *Ḥemdat yamim*.

In that earlier story, a poor man asked Rabbi Isaac for help in preserving himself and his family in life. Rabbi Isaac, however, who had in his hand only a single coin, asked how he could sustain the poor man when that is all he had to give him. The beggar responded that he would add Rabbi Isaac's coin to a coin of the same value that he already had; so Rabbi Isaac gave him the coin. Later the rabbi dreamed that people were attempting to throw him into the sea when the very same poor man to whom he had given the small coin also appeared and brought him safely into the hands of Rabbi Simeon, who had stretched out his hands to save Rabbi Isaac's life. The latter awoke from his dream uttering the verse from Psalms: "Happy is the one who gives thought to the poor; the Lord will deliver him in the day of trouble" (Psalms 41:2).

A comparison with that source in the Zohar points to the literary qualities of the story found in *Ḥemdat yamim*, a very carefully and subtly structured tale that relates to the Sukkot festival on several different levels.

In addition to the association of Abraham with the first evening of Sukkot, the choice of Abraham as the figure in disguise also suggests the connection between Abraham and the virtues of hospitality. In Genesis 18, the patriarch, like the Hasid, welcomes guests into his tent and serves them. The talmudic-midrashic tradition further expanded and accentuated that connection. Hence the biblical personage who exemplified desert hospitality and who, furthermore, served as a prototype of all true hospitality appears in this story in the form of a poor guest who found delight in the deed of the host who walked in his own footsteps in this regard. Moreover, in welcoming the poor man into his *sukkah,* the Hasid extends to him protection from hunger and isolation, which parallels God's protection—as symbolized by the *sukkah*—of the Israelites during the wilderness wanderings.

The dream episode, however, switches the roles, conveying that it is the poor recipient of the hospitality who protects his host. When in the dream, the Hasid asks the identity of the poor guest who saved his life, the latter responds, "I am Abraham *avikha* (your father), adding a personal nuance by the use of a singular suffix. It is as if Abraham were the father, or forefather, of the Hasid, concerned about him as would be a protective, loving parent. And whereas one would expect that it is the poor guest who would be delighted by the wholehearted hospitality, the tale offers another switch—it is the host who rejoices in delight. Indeed, Sukkot is traditionally referred to as the "time of our rejoicing," and the Hasid imbues the joy of that festival with his own meaning: He rejoices because God has sent him a poor man whom he can give the portion of Abraham. Precisely in giving, then, was his joy found.

The tale speaks of "one Hasid," one man of deep and loving piety that expresses itself also in loving relationship to other people. The reader notes that among the group of wise men and scholars (Hakhamim) gathered with him in the *sukkah,* he alone is referred to as Hasid. Furthermore, the Hakhamim are described as being known, whereas the Hasid is not. He is anonymous. In stark contrast to the atmosphere of the sages' feasting in the *sukkah,* is the appearance of a beggar going from house to house asking for a morsel of bread. The Hasid immediately responds to "take the poor man's hand." As his recompense, in the frightful dream in which the Hasid is about to drown in the deep waters, that same poor man "stretched out his hand": measure for measure, a poetic equivalence of deed and reward. Unlike many other stories of this period, which point to the far-reaching consequences of a transgression, this tale illustrates the consequence of a deed of compassion (Stith

Thompson, *Motif-Index of Folk-Literature* [Bloomington, 1955], Q. 42.3: "Generosity to Saint in Disguise Rewarded.")

The reader can also discover a pattern of interrelating verbs and verbal roots in the tale. In the beginning, the Hasid is sitting (*y-sh-v*) in the *sukkah*, while the poor man is referred to as a wandering beggar, *helekh*, and a term derived from the verb *h-l-kh* (to walk). The Hasid immediately rises, takes the beggar's arms, and seats him in the *sukkah*. The beggar, seated along with others present, is, in this sense, no longer to be considered a *helekh:* The host has annulled his guest's status as a stranger and wanderer.

The moment of recognition of the true identity of the beggar occurs in the dream, which contrasts with the earlier scene of jovial fellowship and the sense of security it suggests. Night brings a dream in which the Hasid is utterly alone, in a struggle for his life with the waters of the deep. It is the dream that reveals the inner workings of the story's structure: As grasped in waking experience, the poor guest was dependent upon the almsgiving and hospitality of his host; the dream, however, discloses the deeper and truer relationship between them, one in which the host is actually dependent upon the kindness of his guest.

Inner Intent and Devotion

The Reciter of Psalms

A town is spared from destruction through the
merit of one simple, pious man who is devoted to
the reading of psalms.

In one town there lived a poor man who was also a Hasid. This man, who knew only the simple biblical texts, died at an old age. Within thirty days of his death,[1] he appeared in a dream to another Hasid in that same town and seemed to be standing before him in burial shrouds, holding in his hand a small book.

The second Hasid asked him, "Are you not the person whom we buried on such and such a day?" He said to him, "That is correct. I am that person." And he asked him, "What is that book in your hands?" He answered, "It is the Book of Psalms and I have come to ask you to give warning to the people of this place where I used to live that they might flee from there to save their lives, for evil is about to overtake them. So long as I was alive I completed the reading of the Book of Psalms each week over the course of several years. And for that reason there was peace in this place for a prolonged period, and the people were spared. But from now on there is none to defend them."

In the morning, the second Hasid's spirit was troubled and he sent a messenger to the townspeople to warn them. Indeed, those who held in awe the words of the deceased Hasid fled. But those who doubted the punishment did not heed the words of the Hasid and remained there until the hand of the Lord struck, may the Merciful One spare us.[2]

Ḥemdat yamim, Yamim noraim 6a

1. The second of three stages of the mourning period.
2. Stith Thompson, *Motif-Index of Folk-Literature* (Bloomington, 1955), D. 1810.8.3.1: "Warning in Dream Fulfilled."

This account, included at the end of *Kodesh ḥilulim* (MS, Zentralbibliotek, Zurich 102/19), Avigdor Kara's early-fifteenth-century commentary on Psalm 150, is found also in the epistles of Solomon Shlomel of Dreznitz (published by Simhah-Assaf, *Kovets al yad*, n.s., 3 [1939]:120–121) and in *Emek hamelekh* (Preface, 15a). In all these sources, the account is given a precise time and place: The Hasid lived near the town of Erfurt in Thuringia and the episode is dated

1352, just after the massacre there related to the plague of the Black Death (Gershom Scholem, *Major Trends in Jewish Mysticism* [New York, 1946], 91). The version of the tale translated in this volume is taken from *Ḥemdat yamim*, which does not signify time or place. It appears in that text within a discussion of the practice of reciting psalms during the period of repentance that lasts forty days and culminates in Yom Kippur. The text explains that this practice serves as a defense against punishment: The reading of psalms annuls the very existence of the accusing spirits who bring accusations during that season of divine judgment. One should point out, that *Ḥemdat yamim* advocates this practice for every Jew, the learned person as well as the one unable to engage in more serious forms of study.

The tale consists of a scene preceded and followed by summary statements that stand in sharp contrast to one another. The opening summary represents a long, ongoing period of tranquillity that comes to a close with the death of the devout man, whereas the fatal events of the closing summary statement occur very abruptly. The scene of direct action stands poised between those two statements to convey what is at the very heart of the story: the disclosure that the simple reader of psalms had, in fact, saved his town over a period of many years. As with other such stories from this body of literature, this disclosure occurs in a dream. That literary vehicle is frequently employed to portray a paradoxical view of life and society, to reveal things in their true perspective, one that transcends or even negates society's perceptions. In our tale, even the tranquillity that marked the life-span of the reader of psalms was only an appearance, as danger lurked just beyond the horizon.

If in life the Hasid lacked intellectual knowledge, upon his death he gained access to supernatural knowledge concerning the decree, which he could communicate to the living. But whereas in life his protective activity depended upon himself alone, in death his effort to save the lives of his townspeople depended upon others: upon the sage and Hasid to whom he appeared in a dream and, more crucially, upon the readiness of the villagers to listen and act accordingly. The freedom of response lay no longer in his hands but in theirs.

The reading of psalms is considered to be a very lowly form of religious study, requiring neither rigorous intellectual activity nor even, for that matter, any deep understanding of what one is reading. This story needs to be viewed against the background of the very complex character of the study of the Talmud and its commentaries as it developed in Germany and northern France beginning in the eleventh century. Implicit in the story is the listener's expectation that such a Talmud student might be a more likely figure to save the town from destruction than a man who merely recited psalms.

One need only compare this story with one found in Midrash Tehillim on Psalms 127:1. In the midrash on that verse, "Except the Lord build the house, they who build it labor in vain," it is told that Rabbi Judah ha-Nasi, compiler of the Mishnah, sent a delegation consisting of Rabbi Hiyya, Rabbi Jose, and Rabbi Ammi to visit various cities in the Land of Israel and to arrange there for teachers of Bible and of the Oral Law. Coming to one city in which they found no teachers of either Bible or the Oral Law, they requested that the townspeople bring them the chief watchmen of the city. But when the inhabitants complied and brought the watchmen, the sages explained that these are not the watchmen of the city, that the true watchmen of the city are the teachers of Bible and of the oral tradition.

In contrast to that earlier midrashic account, our study identifies the town's savior with the essentially unlearned Jew, unfortunate in his way and marginal to the life of his community—yet steadfast in his act of reciting psalms. It is significant that the Hasid appears holding not a scholarly volume with long folio pages but, rather, a little book whose very size suggests that it is intended for use by the simple Jew with neither the capacity nor the time for serious study.

The Spilt Oil

A sexton is incapable of pouring oil without
spilling it precisely because he is infatuated
with God.

A Hasid spent much time alone, following the practice of those who separated themselves from worldly matters in order to engage in prayerful solitude. He was completely devoted to God at all times. Once this Hasid came to a town where no one recognized him, and the townspeople appointed him sexton in the synagogue.

And when he prepared oil for the lights, some of the oil spilled, for due to his intense inner preoccupation with God he was unable to pour the oil properly into the oil holders.

But the Hakham[1] (rabbi) of the congregation was able to grasp the real character and quality of the sexton, and he said, "This sexton should really be the Hakham rather than I, and I should serve under him."

Concerning things of this nature it is written, "Be infatuated with love for her always,"[2] for one who loves the Torah so deeply and who cleaves to it with his whole self will err in the things of this world . . .

Reshit Ḥokhmah, Shaar hakedushah 3

1. Sephardic term for rabbi.
2. Proverbs 5:19. The verb suggests the meanings of passion and infatuation and also of error.

Deliverance through a Hallowing Act

Reciting the prayers for sanctification of the moon
with great devotion saves an endangered Jew
from death.

Once a man who was attacked at night by a gentile seeking to kill him requested of the latter that he be able to do one mitzvah before he would die. And seeing that it was the time of the full moon, he recited the sanctification of the moon[1] with greater than usual devotion. A miracle then occurred for him: While jumping three times,[2] as is customary in the rite, the wind raised him up and he was delivered from his enemy.

Ḥemdat yamim, Yamim noraim 49a

    1. The rite in which one blesses the moon's Maker after the new moon is clearly visible in the sky. This is usually done on the Saturday evening following the appearance of the new moon.
    2. While reciting certain words of the rite. See Moses Isserles on the *Shulḥan arukh, Oraḥ ḥayyim* 426:2.

The tale is found in an earlier work on the subject of blessings, *Or ḥadash* (1671) 50c by Benjamin Zeev Bochner, where it is told in the name of Moses Meizlisch of Cracow.

    While the plot of the tale places it in the category of stories of trickery against death or the angel of death, the mood of the tale also transcends this type of tale through its mention of the devotion with which the endangered Jew recited the blessing. The tale thus suggests that it is not simply the fulfillment of the mitzvah in itself but also the degree of devotion accompanying it that accounts for the deliverance.

    The tale is a variant of a more widespread motif—tricking the angel of death by requesting that the intended victim be permitted to perform either a mitzvah or an errand. Compare Stith Thompson, *Motif-Index of Folk-Literature* (Bloomington, 1955), R. 185.1: "A Mortal Deceives Angel of Death." The text in *Or ḥadash* quotes Moses Meizlisch who taught that if one wishes to be saved from a gentile about to kill him, he should simply ask first to be able to fulfill one mitzvah. In this story the moon's brightness (which explains the choice of this particular mitzvah) functions as a sign given by God to the endangered Jew. The granting of the request to fulfill a religious act is a concession to the value system of the Jew; once granted, it gave him the means to be saved from his enemy's threat.

A significant link between the tale and the text of the ceremony seems to be missing in the story as recounted in *Or ḥadash* and in *Ḥemdat yamim*, namely, the words, "As I dance opposite you and am unable to touch you, so may my enemies be unable to touch me for evil purposes," words recited during the rite of sanctification of the moon during the act of jumping three times. We may presume that these words, which date at least from geonic times (*Masekhet sofrim* 19–20), evoked the tale.

Devotion in Prayer

A great sage is praying with such intense
devotion that he is unaware of guests who come to
his house.

Three great sages once came to the house of our teacher and rabbi
Mordecai Masnut—may his memory be for a blessing—a man of great
learning and wealth and piety, in connection with a matter relating to
a mitzvah. Among them was Rabbi Abba Mari—may his memory be
for a blessing. They found Rabbi Masnut sitting upon his knees, his
face directed upward with his hands spread out, reciting the blessing
after meals. So intense was his devotion that he paid no attention to
the learned men who had come to his home; he was unaware even that
anyone had entered.

Then, upon completing his prayer and reciting the final blessing
over a cup of wine, he stood up and greeted his guests, "May your
coming be in peace. Do not regard my oversight as a sin, but forgive
me, for I was engaged in a conversation with my Maker."[1]

Midrash talpiot, Anaf birkat hamazon (Lublin, 1890), 159–160

Rabbi Elijah ha-Kohen (*the Itamari*) quoted this account from *Sefer
keli maḥazik berakhah* (1734) 6a (*Inyan birkat hamazon*) by Israel
Najara. The same story with slight variations in language appears
also in *Ḥemdat yamim* (1763, *Shabbat* 61b).

The situation echoes the talmudic motif of a Hasid praying and
unwilling to interrupt his prayer either to respond to an officer's
greeting (Berakhot 32b–33a, mentioned also in *Sefer ḥasidim* 485
[MS Parma]) or even to care for himself when bitten by a reptile
(Tosefta Berakhot 3:20; see also Berakhot 33a). Our anecdote
differs, however, in two ways: Neither of the older motifs speaks of
the worshiper's being unaware of another's presence due to the
intensity of his prayer; and, whereas in the older talmudic sources
both the officers and the reptile are clearly or potentially alien and
threatening forces, in this story the three scholars are fellow sages
who, as such, represent Rabbi Mordecai's own world of values.

At first sight, the posture of Rabbi Mordecai appears bizarre
and, furthermore, his failure to take notice of the three learned
colleagues could be considered an affront, precisely because of their
learning. Unstated but understood is the concept that a Jew must

show respect to a sage and that even a scholar must show respect to other sages. In this way they express reverence for the Torah, which they have studied and mastered (note Pesaḥim 22b; Makkot 22b; Mishnah Avot 4:15; also "hospitality to guests is greater than welcoming the Divine Presence" [Shabbat 127a]). Upon completing his prayer, Rabbi Mordecai rises to greet his learned colleagues and even asks their forgiveness—suggesting at least the possibility of wrongdoing. That possibility is negated, however, by the total sense of the story; the version in *Ḥemdat yamim* goes so far, even, as to add the words, "And the sages praised him."

Although the code of respect for sages hovers in the background, in this case it is relegated to a secondary status: Instead, one's devotion in prayer, one's relation to God in a life of piety, takes precedence. The values of the Hasid supersede those of the Hakham even when, as in this anecdote, the two coexist in the same person, in a merging of piety and learning that pervades the tale. (Thus although the three visitors are referred to as "great sages," Rabbi Mordecai Masnut himself is referred to as an exceptionally learned man, suggesting a level of erudition that is even higher.) Nevertheless, despite his exemplary scholarly qualities, he is presented essentially as an example not of the class of the Hakham but rather of the Hasid. Even his posture breathes a directness and naïveté that recalls tales of the prayers of the simple, unlettered Jew. His personal piety, which transcends the values of learning itself, serves as the authority for a transvaluation of the commonly accepted ethos.

The paradoxical nuance in this story, the revised estimation of Rabbi Mordecai, is a variant of the type of change that typifies the more normative paradoxical story: In this anecdote, the sage is seen to inhabit an even higher—rather than lower—plane than hitherto believed. Through the eyes of the three visiting scholars, the story discloses another very personal dimension of the sage's life and being—the realm of what transpires purely between man and God, situated beyond society's awareness or perception of him.

The Former
Marrano's Offering

God esteems the misguided but pure intent of a
simple but unlearned man.

In the days of the Ari—may his memory be for a blessing—it once
happened that one of the Marranos[1] who had come from Portugal to
the holy city of Safed in the Upper Galilee—may it be built speedily
in our days—heard the rabbi of that holy community preach concerning the shewbread that was offered in the Temple from week to week.[2]
And it appears that the rabbi sighed during his sermon and, very distressed, said, "And now, due to our many iniquities, we have no such
means to enable the divine abundance to descend upon our world."

Hearing this, that former Marrano went home and, in his wholehearted and simple way, told his wife to prepare for him, at least on
Fridays, two rolls of bread waved thirteen times, kneaded in purity,
beautifully formed, and baked till done in the oven, as he wished to
offer them before the ark of the Lord—perhaps God would favor him
by accepting them and consuming them as a burnt offering. His wife
did just as he had commanded. And each Friday he would bring those
two rolls of bread before the ark of the Lord and would pray and plead
before Him that He willingly accept them and eat them, that He might
find them tasty and fragrant, and so forth, pleading as a child seeking
his father's favor. And he would place the rolls there and leave.

Now the sexton came and took the two rolls without inquiring or
questioning from where they had come or who had brought them, and
he ate them, delighting in them as one rejoices in the yield of the
harvest. Later, at the hour of the evening prayer, that God-fearing man
would run to the ark of the Lord, and as he did not find the rolls his
heart was full of joy and he went and said to his wife, "Praise to God,
may He be blessed, who has not rejected the gift of a poor man, but
has already accepted the bread and has eaten it while it is yet warm.
For the sake of God, be not careless in preparing them, but be very
diligent. For since we have nothing else with which to honor Him and
we note that He delights in these rolls, it is our duty to please Him
with them." And he persisted in this practice for some time.

One Friday it happened that the congregation's rabbi, whose sermon had prompted the man to bring the rolls, was standing at the

61

reading desk reviewing the Sabbath sermon he would deliver the following day, and he saw that man come, as was his good custom, with the rolls and approach the holy ark. The man began to arrange his words and petitions as he was accustomed to do and because of his overflowing enthusiasm and his sense of joy in bringing his present before God he was unaware that the rabbi was standing by the reading desk.

The rabbi remained silent, observing all that the man did and listening to all that he spoke, and then he became angry and called out to him in rebuke, "Idiot! Does our God eat or drink? Beyond any doubt it is the sexton who takes them, while you are of the opinion that it is God who receives them. It is a terrible error to ascribe any corporeality to God—may He be blessed—who has no body and no bodily image." He went on speaking in this manner until the sexton came, as was his custom, to take the rolls. And as the rabbi saw him he called out to him, "Thank this man. Why have you come? And who took the two rolls that this man has been bringing each Friday here in the holy congregation?" The sexton then confessed what he had done.

Upon hearing this, the man who had brought the offering began to cry. And he asked the rabbi to forgive him for he had misunderstood his sermon and thought he was performing a mitzvah, whereas, in truth, according to the rabbi's words, he was actually committing a transgression.

In the aftermath of all this, a special messenger from the Ari—may his memory be for a blessing—came to the rabbi and told him, in the name of holy Rabbi, "Go home and put your affairs in order, for tomorrow during the course of your sermon you shall die. The decree has already gone out concerning this."

The rabbi was terrified. He went to the Ari to inquire of him the nature of his sin and transgression. And the Ari—may his memory be for a blessing—answered him, "I have heard that it is because you withheld pleasure from God. For from that day on which the Temple was destroyed, God has not experienced such delight as when this former Marrano, in the simplicity of his heart, would bring his two rolls and offer them before His ark, thinking that God—may He be blessed—accepted them from him. And because you stopped him from bringing them, it is decreed irrevocably that you shall die."

The rabbi, who had given that sermon, went and put the affairs of his household in order. And on the holy Sabbath, at the time he was to preach, he died, just as the man of God, the Ari—may his memory be for a blessing—had told him.

Mishnat ḥakhamim 220

1. Jews who outwardly had accepted Christianity as a way of avoiding persecution in Spain and Portugal beginning toward the end of the fourteenth century. Also a century later there were those who did so in order to avoid forced emigration with the edicts of expulsion.
2. Leviticus 24:5–9.

Since the meeting of Judaism with Greek and Arabic philosophical thought and especially since Maimonides, it h.., been viewed as a definite religious as well as intellectual flaw to conceive of God in corporeal terms, as having either physical form or attributes. The belief that God "eats" an offering presented to him therefore evoked the sharpest condemnation. While the premises of the above story regard a corporeal concept as a severe wrong, the legend conveys that it is even worse for the learned to allow their greater knowledge and wisdom to make mockery of a naïve and misguided act of devotion. The latter would exemplify the pitfall of pride on the part of the sage, and the severity of the sentence affirms the gravity of that offense. It is noteworthy that this story found within a book directed toward the learned Jew (consider the very title), extols the inner intent of a simple, devout Jew even in such an extreme and bizarre situation. The underlying formula emerges that God takes greater delight in a naïve deed of devotion—even a heretical one— than in the much more sophisticated wisdom represented by the rabbi in the story, a preference expressed in the imposition of the very harsh decree even though the rabbi was, in fact, not even aware of the implications of his censuring the unlearned converso.

The general pattern of the story is present in an anecdote mentioned in Elijah ben Solomon ha-Kohen's *Shevet musar* 34 (1712). In discussing the role of the *sheliaḥ tsibur*, the one who leads the congregation in prayer, the author, a famous rabbi in Smyrna, quotes an episode that he had heard from a relative, Rabbi Abraham Apumadu: "In former years, there was a *sheliaḥ tsibur* of very advanced age. When he read from the Torah scroll, he would make movements with his hand to allude to the happenings in the reading. He did this for many years. Once a rabbi came there and, regarding these antics as shameful, put a stop to them. Then, in a terrifying dream, the rabbi was informed that one man who had brought honor and joy to the Holy One, blessed be He, was now prevented from doing so. At dawn, the rabbi immediately went to the home of the *sheliaḥ tsibur* to ask his forgiveness and to request that he resume his hand movements."

Note also the similarity to the tale of the herdsman's prayer in *Sefer ḥasidim* 5–6 (MS Parma). It deals not with an unnormative act per se but with an unnormative way of praying on the part of an unlearned shepherd who is, nonetheless, deeply devout in his religious feeling.

Tamar Alexander ("Demuto shel haari basippur hasefaradi-yehudi," *Peamim*, 26 [1986]: 87–107) traces the development of the story type found in "The Former Marrano's Offering" from a moral tale to a hagiographical story as it becomes attached to the biographical legend of the Ari. The story in its legendary mode also appears in the Ladino midrash *Meam loaz*, within the section on Joshua, which was written considerably after *Mishnat ḥakhamim*. In this process, Alexander points out, the element of the protest of the lower social class against the religious establishment is lost because the hero of the legendary story, the Ari, is himself in the category of a religious leader. She cites sources that indicate that the essential story, lacking any connection with a historical figure as hero, had already existed in the period prior to the expulsion of Jews from Spain, and in those earlier versions it was also unrelated to the phenomenon of Marranos.

From the Sensuous to God

Through his single-minded infatuation with the physical beauty of a princess, a man grows gradually more and more detached from the sensuous and develops the same single-minded obsession with God.

One day, as the princess stepped out of her bath, one of the idlers saw her and, sighing deeply, said, "Oh, would that she were mine that I might make love to her." And the princess answered him, "In the cemetery such will be the case." Hearing these words, he was very glad, thinking she had told him to go to the cemetery to wait there until she came to him, that they might lie together. Actually, she did not mean that at all. She was merely indicating that in death there is equality between small and great, young and old, between the most common and the most honored ones—all these will be equal. But here and now such is not the case. Indeed it is considered improper for a commoner to have intimate relations with a princess.

The man rose and went to the cemetery and he sat there, and he thought only of her as he continuously contemplated her form. Out of his deep desire for her, his thought became more abstract and removed from the sensuous. Day and night, sitting in the cemetery, he thought only of the woman's form and her beauty. There he ate and drank and slept, for he thought that if today she does not come, then surely tomorrow she will.

In his solitude, he focused all of his thoughts on the one object with such a degree of single-mindedness that his soul came to be liberated from the sensual. He came to be attached instead to mental concepts to the point of being completely detached from the sensual, even from the woman. And he cleaved to God—may He be blessed— attaining that state in which all sensual things are removed from his consciousness. And his great desire was in the divine idea, and he became a man of God, so completely devoted to God that his prayer was heard above and his blessing had effect for all passersby. And merchants and knights and pilgrims passing along that way would turn to him to receive his blessing, and he became known even in distant places.

Reshit ḥokhmah, Shaar haahavah, end of chapter 4

Elijah de Vidas included this story in his treatise in the name of Rabbi Isaac of Acre (a noted Kabbalist of the late thirteenth through mid-fourteenth centuries), and he continued to quote from the latter: "One having no passionate desire for a woman is likened to a donkey or even worse, the reason being that from what one experiences sensually a person must proceed to understand the service of God," serving Him with the same quality of passion. Intensity of sensual desire, it would appear, is a gateway—perhaps even an indispensable gateway—to religious passion. This parable suggests the influence of Platonic thought, possibly transmitted through the channel of the mystical Sufi tradition of Islam.

The Disclosure
of Hidden Truth

A False Accusation is Disproved

The truth becomes evident, while the accusation of the mob is disproved.

It occurred in Spain that gentiles came [to the royal court] saying that on the day before Passover a slain person had been found in the house of a Jewish man. One of the king's advisers and ministers spoke harshly against the holy people of Israel, and the people further pressed their demand before the king, warning that if he did not execute justice, then they would take matters into their own hands to avenge the blood that had been shed. The king responded, "May the true Ruler who judges in righteousness, the God of trust, lacking iniquity, be exulted and praised. And now I will show you your lies and those of my adviser. And you, relate to your children that which you will see."

He then summoned all the Jews to appear before him, and when they came he asked them, "What is the meaning of David's words, 'Behold He that guards Israel neither slumbers nor sleeps'?[1] For if He does not slumber, all the more so it is understood that He does not sleep, for in the holy tongue sleep is more than slumber." The Jews responded with explanations taken from the commentators to the effect that it is the way of the biblical text to speak in this manner: He does not slumber, and all the more so, then, it is that He does not sleep.

But the king asked, "Can a question be answered by repeating the same question? And if you do not understand, I do understand now as a result of what I beheld with my own eyes, for last night I could neither slumber nor sleep; sleep was withheld from my eyes. And I rose from my bed and went to the outer courtyard and looked out the window. The moonlight was very bright and I saw men running, and I saw upon the shoulder of one of them something that resembled a human corpse. So I sent three men to follow them without revealing themselves to ascertain if it was, in fact, a slain person and to inform me. And my servants whom I had so commanded went and situated themselves in a hiding place. They saw that it was a slain person, and they recognized two of the men carrying that corpse. And here are the witnesses before you."

The men came and testified, and the king's adviser questioned the witnesses. "Why didn't you grab them?" he asked. They responded that those whom they were observing hurriedly threw the corpse into the courtyard of the Jew and fled; furthermore the culprits were bearing arms, whereas they, the witnesses, were unarmed as the king had not commanded them to take the men but simply to observe what was occurring.

As they finished speaking, the king then returned to his subject and said, "This is what Scripture says, 'The Guardian of Israel neither slumbers nor sleeps,' meaning, He who guards Israel does not slumber and, in addition, does not allow others to sleep."

The mob, then, left in utter despair, and those who plotted the libel were punished . . .

Ḥemdat yamim, Moadim 25a

1. Psalms 121:4.

This account is found already in Solomon ibn Verga, *Sefer shevet yehuda* (Jerusalem, 1947), 62–63, written shortly after the expulsion from Spain. It is found also in *Sefer shalshelet hakabbalah* by Gedalia ibn Yahya (Abraham David, "The Historiographical Work of Gedalya ibn Yahya, Author of 'Shalshelet hakabbalah' " [Ph.D. diss., Hebrew University, 1976], 84), where the king in the tale is identified as Alfonso XI who ruled Castile from 1322 to 1350. Transferred to a Turkish context, the same story also appears in Moses Gaster, ed., *Maaseh Buch* vol. 2 (Philadelphia, 1934), no. 185.

The events related by the king recall the biblical Book of Esther. There, too, the king, Ahasuerus, is unable to sleep, and his sleeplessness leads to the salvation of the endangered Jews in his realm. The account set in Spain offers a variation on those belonging to a larger family of tales about the miraculous or near-miraculous means by which the truth is proved in cases of blood libel: The truly guilty are exposed and the Jewish community is saved from the mob. Note Gaster, *Maaseh Buch*, vol. 2, no. 171.

In addition to the obvious setting of this account at the beginning of the Passover festival and its component of blood (Exodus 12), more subtle allusions connect the narrative with the festival and the biblical account of the Exodus from Egypt. The king orders the mob to tell (*h-g-d, haggadah*) their children what they see just as the Israelites were commanded to tell their children of the deliverance from bondage (Exodus 13:8). The passage concludes with mention of judgments (*shefatim*), a word used for the punishments that God meted out to the Egyptian oppressors (Exodus 12:12). In the tale, those judgments, executed by the king on the basis of testimony and empirical fact, make an oblique mockery of the mob's impassioned plea for justice in the absence of trustworthy testimony.

The enmity of the mob, eagerly drawing hostile conclusions and ready to act upon them, contrasts with the king, whose pious attitude goes hand in hand with his being a protector of the friendless Jews in his kingdom. The roles of these three protagonists quite obviously mirror perceptions of the sympathy and hostility of king and mob respectively.

Despite the thrust of this particular tale, the broader context of *Hemdat yamim* blurs the contrast between mob and king. There the account is said to exemplify many such episodes in which "our enemies and those who seek evil for us" play a crucial part in saving the Jews from that very evil. Even Ahasuerus is mentioned as one who, though he despised Jews no less than did Haman himself, nevertheless had a role in saving them from the fate that he would otherwise have wished upon them. One might speculate that the tragic events connected with the expulsion from Spain altered perceptions of the relations between the king of a Christian land and his Jewish subjects.

The Remarkable Fig Tree

A wondrous tree discloses a hidden crime.

Rabbi Solomon Alkabez[1] was thoroughly familiar with both mystic teaching and grammar, and he composed many liturgical poems [*piyyutim*]. But his great wisdom evoked envy on the part of the enemies of the Jews, and an Ishmaelite once lay in wait for him and murdered him and buried him in his garden near a fig tree. It happened that the fig tree began to blossom considerably before its time,[2] and it produced such large and beautiful figs that all the townspeople were amazed.

Report of the tree was brought to the attention of the Muslim king. And when the king saw those fruits, he, too, was amazed and sent for that Ishmaelite and inquired of him how he was able to bring his fruits to such an early ripening. The Arab, struck with fear, was unable even to answer the king, and his silence provoked the king to afflict him with hard and bitter punishments until he had no choice but to confess. For from the very day on which he had killed Rabbi Solomon Alkabez, the Jew, that tree began to grow fruit before its time. The king ordered that the Arab murderer be hanged on that very tree.

Kav hayashar 86:3–4

1. Kabbalist and poet (ca. 1505–1576) who immigrated to Safed and whose poem *Lekha dodi* was incorporated into the liturgy for the welcoming of the Sabbath.
2. Stith Thompson, *Motif-Index of Folk-Literature* (Bloomington, 1955), D. 2145.2.2.2: "Tree Blossoms Out of Season," and E. 631.0.5: "Tree from Innocent Man's Blood."

The same legend, almost word for word, is found in *Shalshelet hakabbalah* of Gedalia ibn Yahye, which appeared in Venice in 1585/1586. In that work the legend relates to the eleventh-century Spanish Hebrew poet, Solomon ibn Gabirol. See Abraham David, "The Historiographical Work of Gedalya ibn Yahya, Author of Shalshelet hakabbalah" [Ph.D. diss., Hebrew Uniersity, 1976], p. 89. The legend was thus transferred in its entirety to a later subject. Although the poet has no active role in either text, the story nonetheless praises his poetic genius with the symbol of the beautiful tree. That genius and the beauty defy all attempts to annihilate them, as truth is disclosed and triumphs over the attempt to conceal it beneath the ground.

The Torah Reading
Disproves a Lie

The Torah itself can foil an attempt at deception.

It happened in the days of the Rabbi (the Ari)—may his memory be for a blessing—that he commanded his students not to write down that which they hear from him. He gave no permission to write down his words except to our teacher Rabbi Hayyim Vital, the only one who truly grasped his teaching.[1] But even so, each one would take down his words in writing, until one day he called Rabbi M. Meshulum[2] to the reading of the Torah for the verse, "And Moses wrote the book, and so forth."[3] When the student descended from the reading desk he came to kiss the Rabbi's hands.[4] The latter said to him, "Did I not tell you that you are not to write what you hear from me?" And he answered, "My master, from the day you commanded us, we have not written." The Ari asked him, "And does the Torah, God forbid, lie? For you read in it, 'And Moses wrote.'"

The student was dumbfounded by this and could not respond.

Ḥemdat yamim, Shabbat 80a

1. See *Emek hamelekh*, Introduction, 11b.
2. In line with manuscripts of *Toledot haari*, David Tamar suggests that the name is a copyist's error for Moses *mashlim* (the one who completes the Torah reading, namely the seventh person called to the Torah (David Tamar, *Meḥkarim betoledot hayehudim beerets yisrael uveitalia* [Jerusalem, 1970], 187).
3. Deuteronomy 31:9.
4. According to the Sephardic custom following one's reading from the Torah scroll.

The same legend, in somewhat different form, appears in *Shivḥei haari* (Lvov, 1849), 2ab; also *Sefer hakavanot umaase nissim* (Constantinople, 1720), 4ab; and Meir Benayahu, *Sefer toledot haari* (Jerusalem, 1967), 163–164, no. 10.

The textual context in *Ḥemdat yamim* reinforces the belief that the portion of the Torah that a person is called to read contains a message to him from God, specifically a sign for self-scrutiny including a disclosure of what one himself conceals. The Ari's function here is only as an interpreter of that more "objective" sign.

The respectful and affectionate practice of kissing the master's hands after being called to the Torah reading is followed by the sharp contrast between the expected and the actual response on the part of the Ari. As in other forms of the Ari's wondrous knowledge, the disclosure serves as conclusive proof of guilt. The Ari's proof, based in this case upon the Torah reading, penetrates to the secrets of the self and unmasks hidden sins, demolishing all protective barriers that cover up the misdeed.

This legend might reflect the tension between the Ari's desire to limit knowledge of his mystical teachings to the circles of his students and the dissemination of his teachings throughout the Jewish world in the decades following his death in 1572. It is known, in fact, that three years after he died, his students signed an oath that none would convey to anyone outside the group that which Rabbi Hayyim Vital would teach them of Luria's teachings— except with Vital's permission (Gershom Scholem, "Shtar hahitkashrut shel talmidei haari," *Zion* 5 [1940]: 125, 241ff.). The explanation also circulated that because he had disclosed so many mystical teachings, it was decreed on high that the Ari must die at a much earlier age than would otherwise have been the case (*Emek hamelekh* [1648], Introduction, 11b).

An Agitating Dream

*Inadvertent wrongdoing brings on a
disturbing dream.*

A man who practiced a superior level of repentance during the Ten
Days of Repentance[1] dreamed one night during those ten days that his
feet were filthy with dung. His spirit was agitated[2] by his desire to
know the meaning of his dream. He recounted his dream to the Rabbi
(the Ari)—may his memory be for a blessing for the life of the world
to come—who answered him, "Your soul is not pure, for you have not
conducted yourself in purity in that your bed was close to the bed upon
which your wife lay in her menstrual state.[3] And while you were sleeping at night your pillow actually touched your wife's bed while she was
in her menstrual state." That man went and examined the matter and
found the words of the Rabbi—may his memory be for a blessing for
the life of the world to come—to be true.

Ḥemdat yamim, Yamim noraim 49b

1. From Rosh Hashanah through Yom Kippur.
2. Genesis 41:8, in reference to Pharaoh's dreams.
3. An extension of the prohibition of sexual intercourse during the woman's
menstrual state (Leviticus 18:19).

The legend reflects the belief that any flaw in one's state of purity
might be mirrored in one's dreams; that is, the nature of a dream
reflects the state of the soul. The latter is in turn influenced by the
individual's deeds, willful or unwillful, including even those of which
he might himself be unaware. "At times God sends a bad dream to
awaken a person to repentance" (*Reshit ḥokhmah, Shaar hateshuvah*
1). Also *Kav hayashar* 17:3, in a passage that refers to this same
incident, quotes the Ari as saying that dreams generally come to
inform a person of some iniquity on his part.

The Trembling of a Hasid

Spiritual distress of a devout man.

One day a Hasid was seen shouting and weeping and striking his face and uttering words of confession with a bitter voice. When asked the reason for his great trembling, he answered that in a certain place on that very day, one who shared the root of the Hasid's soul had abandoned Judaism for another religion. This brought him untold distress, for he recognized that consequently his own soul was not in a state of purity.

Ḥemdat yamim, Yamim noraim 69a

Although the reader assumes a clear distinction between the faithful Hasid and the convert who has betrayed the covenant, the anecdote erases any such dichotomy. It conveys the message that a sin on the part of another person affects oneself and might even reflect a part of oneself.

The notion that there are those who belong to the root of one's soul is a mystic concept that refers to people who are spiritually related and hence interdependent. Hence the apostasy of one so spiritually related—though he might be a total stranger—discloses something about one's own soul and its hidden tendencies, its lack of wholeness and purity. A sin on the part of one so interrelated leaves its stain upon one's own soul. The same concept of soul-relatedness —connected with the idea of the place of one's soul within the soul of Adam, which contained all souls—becomes important in eighteenth-century Hasidism and its theory of the Tzaddik, the central figure of a hasidic community, who shares, on a mental or spiritual level, the sin of his followers. Because they share the same soul-root, he can thus help them to repair and redeem that sin.

With the context of *Ḥemdat yamim*, this tale relates to the need of the Jew to seek atonement on Yom Kippur not only for himself and his household but also for all those who, to any degree, share his own soul-root or who share any other aspect of his soul, as delineated in kabbalistic teaching.

The Living and the Dead

The Oath That Could Not Be Fulfilled

The deceased, despite their intentions and promises, are unable to reveal to the living their experience in death.

Rabbenu Jehiel, the father of Rabbenu Asher,[1] had a friend in his city who, like him, was exceedingly devout. The two very dear friends were both elderly men of deeds who exemplified high levels of both learning and piety. They took a mutual oath that the first to die would appear in his friend's dream to tell him what occurs in death and to reveal the path of the soul upon death.[2]

On the day that his friend died, when Rabbenu Jehiel was in the cemetery prior to the burial, he stood and said to those assembled, "Listen, my masters, my friend who lies here dead before me and I took an oath together, and so I remind him, in your presence, to fulfill his oath." Then everyone noticed that the deceased's coffin was shaking somewhat, and they opened his coffin thinking that the dead one may have come back to life. But only his eyelashes moved, and it was agreed by all that the blinking of his eyes was a sign that he was unable to disclose anything.

Nevertheless, thirty days later, the deceased Hasid came and appeared to the rabbi, Rabbenu Jehiel, requesting his forgiveness concerning the oath, for he was not permitted to tell him anything.

Kav hayashar 88:4–5

1. Talmudist, legal codifier, and rabbi in Toledo, Spain (ca. 1250–1327), and known as Rosh.
2. Compare Stith Thompson, *Motif-Index of Folk-Literature* (Bloomington, 1955), "Return of the Dead to Keep Promise and Tell of Land of the Dead," variation of E. 374.1 and M. 252.

Death is sensed as a boundary that human knowledge may not penetrate. Even an oath, which in Jewish law has most serious implications in binding a person to fulfill his word, cannot penetrate that boundary. Death, however, is not a wall of "deadness." For the deceased displays signs of life in communicating that he will not communicate what he had promised: not that he is unable to but rather that he is not permitted to do so.

Father Abraham Completes a Prayer Quorum

*The biblical patriarch notes the great distress of
his descendants at being unable to pray as a
congregation on the holiest day of the year, and
he appears to complete the necessary quorum for
prayer.*

It was the case in Hebron, long ago, that a quorum of ten Jews required
to hold public worship[1] was not always found, except on the Sabbath
and holy days, when people from the villages would gather there to
pray. Nevertheless the inhabitants of Hebron exemplified the highest
level of piety. Once, when it was almost time to begin the prayers of
Yom Kippur there were only nine men in Hebron. They waited for
the villagers to come, but not one of them came for they had all gone
up to Jerusalem instead. The Jews of Hebron were thus very distressed
at the thought that on Yom Kippur they would not be able to pray
together as a congregation. And there was much weeping.

Looking out as the sun was just about to set,[2] they beheld a very
old man, whom they were exceedingly glad to see. When he approached they offered him a meal before the fast, but he simply blessed
them and explained, "I've already eaten along the way." They wor-
shiped on the holy day and treated the man with great respect. At the
end of the day they began quarreling among themselves because each
person wished to invite the guest to his house. They decided to cast
lots, and the winner was the *ḥazzan*,[3] a truly devout man who could
disclose wondrous things in dreams and visions. The *ḥazzan* walked
home with the guest following him. Upon reaching his home, however,
when the *ḥazzan* turned around to honor his guest by having him
enter first, the guest was not to be found anywhere in the courtyard.

That night, however, the old man appeared to the *ḥazzan* in a
dream to inform him that he was Abraham[4] our father—may he rest
in peace—who had come into their midst to be the tenth man, to
complete the prayer quorum, for he had seen their distress at not being
able to pray as a congregation.

They rejoiced and praised God who related to them so wondrously.

Kol sasson 4

1. Ten Jews are necessary to comprise a *minyan*, a quorum for praying together as a congregation.
2. The worship and fast of Yom Kippur (the Day of Atonement) begins prior to sundown and continues until the onset of darkness the following evening.
3. The person leading the chanting of the liturgy.
4. According to Genesis 25, Abraham is among those buried at the Cave of Machpelah in Hebron.

This legend is found also in *Emek hamelekh* (1648), Introduction, 14a–14b. It demonstrates that the bonds of concern are stronger and more real than death. In this legend, the patriarch's concern and compassion for his descendants manifests itself in his returning to the world as an old man. He does not reveal his identity until later, leaving open the possibility that any anonymous elderly person might be such a messenger from the "world of truth."

Souls in Exile

The Ari is able to perceive the presence of
wandering souls in a state of exile and also
to repair their condition, bringing them to a
state of rest.

The earth's atmosphere is full of souls in exile, those not yet permitted to attain a state of rest.

Once the Ari—may his memory be for a blessing—who had gone out to the field to study Torah, noted that all the trees there were full of souls beyond number. The same was true of the field, and similarly myriads of souls were upon the waters. When the Rabbi, the Ari, inquired of them what they were doing there, they responded that they had been cast out beyond the holy veil for they had not repented of their wrongdoings. And, further, they were even making it difficult for their friends to repent. Consequently they were wandering, ceaselessly, upon the earth or in the atmosphere all about. But they had heard a heavenly voice announcing throughout the worlds that there is one man, a righteous and saintly person in the land, the Ari—may his memory be for a blessing—who has the power to repair the exiled souls. For this reason the souls had gathered here to entreat him to have compassion on them and to mend them so that they might come to their place of rest rather than having to go on suffering as they were.

The Ari, that Hasid, promised to do whatever was possible to help them. Afterward he spoke of this encounter with his students, who had noted that their master was voicing questions, but they had not known with whom he was actually conversing.

And in his composition it is written that those souls could ascend by means of the prayer of a saintly person, for when a saintly one prays with true devotion his prayer ascends to the very Throne of God. And so several souls clad themselves in his prayer to accompany it on its way upward.[1]

Kav hayashar 5:4–7

---

1. Concerning the Ari's welcoming of the Sabbath, *Hemdat yamim* (1763) *Shabbat* 38b mentions, in addition, that "amidst the great tumult and the coming together of countless souls, his eyesight almost dimmed from seeing all this and he had to close his eyes, but doing so he still beheld them with his eyes closed." See also *Emek hamelekh* (1648), Introduction, 11a.

The ascending and descending of souls is explained in the ensuing discussion in *Ḥemdat yamim:* Even souls cloaked in the shells of impurity, the antithesis of the divine, long to ascend to realms of holiness and must stand in judgment to be allowed entrance. Those descending are the additional souls given to each righteous person on the Sabbath. The subject of wandering souls that are barred from any resting place until their tasks are completed, is found in the Zohar (3:127a). See also Zohar 3:180a.

The Dybbuk¹ and the Unbelieving Woman

A spirit that enters a woman's body because of her secret disbelief departs when she affirms her belief in the Exodus.

In the days of our Rabbi, the Ari—may his memory be for a blessing for the life of the world to come—it once happened that a spirit entered into a woman, causing her great distress. And when her relatives noted the extent of her pain they entreated the Rabbi to save her. He then sent our teacher, Hayyim Vital, who went to the woman and asked the spirit numerous questions concerning himself and the reason that he was punished in this way. And the spirit told him that he was being punished for his sin with a married woman and for bringing into existence the offspring of an adulterous union. Rabbi H. Vital went on to inquire of the spirit concerning the iniquity of the woman, which enabled him to enter into her body. And the spirit responded that this happened to the woman because her true self is not as it appears. She did not believe in the Exodus from Egypt. And on the evening of Passover when all Israel rejoices in gladness, reciting the Hallel² and relating the going out from Egypt, all this is as a laughing matter in her eyes for she thinks that this miracle never occurred.

The rabbi's heart sank, as he could barely believe what he had heard. He trembled at hearing of her evil heart and said to her, "Have you not lost your hope? Behold you are as one of the pagan women, and for that reason this distress has come upon you and you are totally lost.³ Only if you will believe in perfect faith that the Holy One, blessed be He, created the heavens and the earth and that He has the capacity to do all that He desires and none can question Him concerning His doings⁴ can you be freed from this situation." She responded with the words, "Yes, I believe completely."

He continued, asking the woman, "Do you believe that the Holy One, blessed be He, brought us out from Egypt and split the sea for us?" And the woman said, "Amen, amen." The rabbi continued, asking her, "Do you believe all this in perfect faith and do you repent with a complete repentance?" And he evoked in her remorse and regret⁵ concerning her prior sins. The woman answered "Yes" and began to cry.

And so the rabbi pronounced a decree concerning that spirit, and it departed from her and went on its way.[6]

Ḥemdat yamim, Moadim 24a

1. The belief that a deceased and doomed soul seeks habitation in the body of a living person can be traced to the literature of the Second Temple period (witness accounts in the Gospels). The idea acquired significance in connection with the belief in metempsychosis in Lurianic Kabbalah. It was held that souls with especially grave sins were not permitted even the option of transmigration and so, without any place of rest, they sought a haven within the body of a living person—something that could occur only if the one into whom the spirit entered was guilty of a secret sin. See Gershom Scholem, *Kabbalah* (Jerusalem, 1974), 349; and Hayyim Vital, *Shaar hagilgulim* (Frankfurt Am Main, 1684).

2. Psalms of praise (Psalms 113–118) recited on joyous festivals of the year, including Passover.

3. The words taken from Deuteronomy 32:36.

4. Words taken from the traditional death confession.

5. The words, with another meaning, are found in Exodus 32:4.

6. She is now witness to the departure of the evil spirit from her body (*yetsiat hadybbuk*), which parallels the miracle of the going forth from Egypt (*yetsiat mitsrayim*) in which she had previously expressed disbelief. Her act of belief in the departure from Egypt makes possible the departure of the dybbuk.

From Man to Ox

A son redeems his father's soul from being
tortured as a beast and enables it to
transmigrate back into a human being.

It once happened in Castile that gentiles had designated an ox for sport, it being their custom to beat and afflict an animal. During the night preceding the event a Jew had a dream in which he saw his father, who told him, "Know, my son, that because of my many iniquities I transmigrated into an ox following my death, and it is the very ox designated for affliction and hard blows tomorrow in the people's sport.

"And so, my son, redeem me and save me that I may flee through a certain place before they kill me by tearing me to pieces alive. Redeem me from their hands: Give no thought to the cost involved, and slaughter the ox in a proper manner and feed it to poor students of Torah.

"I have been informed of this from above and have been permitted to inform you. In this way my soul shall ascend, returning from transmigration into an animal to transmigration into a human being and enabling me to serve the Lord, with God's help."

Sefer ḥaredim 3:7

This tale, found also in *Ḥemdat yamim* (1763) *Yamim noraim* 56a, opposes a pair of antithetical value systems: the world of the Spanish sport with its practices of physically tormenting animals and that of feeding poor students. The polarity, furthermore, contrasts meat that is *terefah* (nonkosher, literally an animal torn into pieces while still alive) and the meat of an animal properly slaughtered according to ritual procedure (*sheḥitah*). Thus the ox as entertainment symbolizes the values of Spanish society, whereas the antithetical Jewish values include redemption (*pidyon*), proper ritual slaughter, almsgiving, and Torah study. Only the values of the latter, embodied in the son's act of redeeming his father's soul, can restore the father from an animal to a human level of existence.

Again we see that appearances are not identical with truth. But metempsychosis can expose hidden truths regarding one's true nature and acts: A return to life in the form of an animal alludes to the morally subhuman nature of one's hidden deeds.

This story and the ones that immediately follow voice much of the mystery and dread implicit in the concept of metempsychosis, namely, the sense that everyone and everything might be, in truth, something else, that any and every beast might house the soul of a person requiring *tikkun*. A decidedly paradoxical sense of reality emerges: Beyond the reality of our world as it appears to human eyes lies a complex nexus of the identities of humans and of all other forms of life. This otherworldly reality is disclosed either through the wondrous knowledge of the mystic hero or in dreams. The dread of this kind of realization easily invited Kafka to give it new form in his famous story "Metempsychosis."

Ḥemdat yamim, in the discussion preceding this story, states that "most of the souls of the latter generations have transmigrated and have come now to repair what they did not mend in the beginning."

Retribution for the Wrongs of a Previous Life

A bizarre example of metempsychosis and its mysterious ways of justice.

A student of the Torah, desiring to travel to a certain place, came before the Ari to request that he write a letter on his behalf. The Rabbi said to him, "I will do as you have requested. And go there, for the Lord, your God, has brought it about that there you will find your life partner."

The young man went to that place, where they greatly honored him. One of the wealthy men among the town's residents gave his daughter to him as a wife and gave him a generous dowry and many gifts. Then, three months later, the wife died.

The Rabbi explained the secret of that matter: The woman had been the soul of a man who, in a prior life, had been a business partner of this husband. He had made a false accusation against him and had taken money from him. Because he had caused him distress for a period of about three months, the student now enjoyed the woman's beauty for an equivalent period of time, and in place of the money the student had then lost, he acquired his wife's inheritance.

All the students responded in exclaiming, "Great is the design, and so forth,[1] for Your eyes are open to observe all the ways of human beings and to give to each person according to the fruits of his own doings."

Ḥemdat yamim, Yamim noraim 53a

1. Jeremiah 32:19.

A somewhat different version of the same story is found in Meir Benayahu, *Sefer toledot haari* (Jerusalem, 1967), 177–178, no. 20.

What appears totally perplexing to the student is, as perceived by the Ari, a clear, albeit complex, enactment of justice that crosses the boundaries of individual and sexual identity to have an impact on the joys and pains of life. Justice is meted out with mathematical precision.

From Man to Dog:
The Reincarnation of Sin

*A fierce dog who attacked a woman is seen to
bear the avenging soul of a man whom she had
enticed to sin.*

In the days of the Ari it once happened that a dog was greatly excited
about a certain man's house and would constantly encompass it. It was
a black dog of terrifying appearance that frightened people, for its face
resembled that of a demon. And although the man repeatedly drove
the dog away with sticks, the dog would still return. Indeed, every
single morning the man found the dog standing near the entrance
waiting for someone to open the door so that it could then force its
way into the house. As many times as the man drove out the dog,
ordering that the door be closed after it, the dog nevertheless returned
and waited at the door until it was opened again.

All this happened repeatedly until one day that man did not remember to close the door behind him. The dog entered the house and
bounded from room to room until it came to the bed of that man's
wife's bed. Finding her still asleep, the dog jumped onto the bed and
bit her several times, leaving a fresh wound and bruises before running
off. The woman gave out such a terrible and bitter cry that all the town
moaned at its sound.

And at the same time, the Rabbi explained the secret of the matter,
namely, that this woman had slept with her neighbor, who had since
died, and his soul entered into this dog. And because this woman,
through her glib speech, had enticed him to have intimate relations
with her, the dog now came to exact revenge.

Afterward, they made the woman swear to tell the truth, and she
acknowledged the truth of all that the Rabbi had spoken.

Ḥemdat yamim, Yamim noraim 56a

Note Meir Benayahu, *Sefer toledot haari* (Jerusalem, 1967), 237 n. 2,
for further sources in which this story appears. In *Kav hayashar*
34:3–11, this episode appears within a larger narrative context.
There the husband is identified as Abraham ibn Pedah, a devout and
generous man. The neighbor, a merchant, fell ill and died after

gradual physical decay. Some years later the Hasid would find the black dog at his doorstep when he left for the synagogue in the morning as well as when he returned home. In that source, the story contains an epilogue in which the woman, after confessing her adultery, repented and died in a state of repentance. But upon learning of her unfaithfulness, the Hasid imediately divorced her; that is, after driving away (*g-r-sh*) the dog, he divorced (*g-r-sh*) his wife. Compare Stith Thompson, *Motif-Index of Folk-Literature* (Bloomington, 1955), B. 134.1: "Dog Betrays Woman's Infidelity."

From Affliction to Rest

A student who witnesses a scene of affliction is able, through tikkun, *to bring the afflicted to a state of rest.*

One day the sage Rabbi Jacob Abulafia[1] came before my teacher (the Ari)—may his memory be for a blessing. My master spoke first and said to him, "Your honor wants to go to Egypt and requests of me that I write a letter for him." And Abulafia answered, "Yes, it is so, my master." The Ari continued, "May my master go in peace and may the Lord be with you on your journey. Indeed, great benefit will come of your going there because it is a matter of great necessity."

He asked him, "What is the necessity?"—this was, after all, a journey of his own choosing! The Ari responded, "Upon your safe return you will surely fathom my words." My master immediately wrote the letter on his behalf and gave it to him, warning him yet again concerning this matter and urging him to proceed quickly with his journey. And so he did.

He set out and journeyed to Egypt where he was greatly honored out of respect for the Rabbi and for himself. Afterward he set out to return home to Safed—may it be built and established quickly in our days. He left with a caravan, and all that the others in the group did he also did. One day the members of the caravan were resting as was their custom, and that sage also rested. And as he got down from the donkey, a deep sleep immediately came over him and he slumbered for about an hour. When the others got up to go they woke the sage from his sleep. He arose and untied the donkey, and the donkey strayed. And again the wise man was overcome by deep sleep and slept about two hours. Seeing no one when he awoke, he shuddered and shook and began to run about in a state of trembling and great distress.

As evening approached he saw a plower and oxen coming into view. He rejoiced and thought, "I will go with them," and he ran toward them. On reaching the site, he noticed that the plower was cruelly beating the oxen. A little while later he saw that the plower had turned into an ox and the ox had become a man who placed a burden upon the other and began to beat him harshly. This continued for some time. The sage was terrified. He had no place to flee since he did not know where he might find an inhabited place,[2] and he was exceedingly agitated because he could make no sense of any of this.

91

Then, when the sun went down, all three of them became humans and cried. And they spoke to the sage saying, "Welcome, do you come from Safed?" He answered them, "Yes." They then inquired of him, "Does Rabbi Isaac Luria Ashkenazi live in Safed?" Again he answered, "Yes." They fell at his feet weeping, and the wise man also wept with them. And they asked him, "Has my master seen our affliction and our distress?" He responded that he had. Then they said to him, "For the sake of the Holy One of Israel, please have mercy upon us, for we are of the people Israel. When you return to Safed, quickly go before the Rabbi and fall down before him and plead with him to mend our souls because you see that all our strength is gone and we are desperate.[3]

The sage said, "I will indeed do as you have requested," and they made him take an oath of a grave nature to fulfill every act of *tikkun*[4] that the Rabbi would prescribe on their behalf. Then, in the twinkling of an eye, the sage found himself back in the caravan, his spirit revived.

Upon arriving in Safed, he immediately came to the Rabbi to plead with him on behalf of those misfortunate ones. But the Rabbi spoke first: "I know that it is because of the matter of the oxen that my master comes to me. Return tomorrow." And he did so.

And my teacher—may his memory be for a blessing—said to him, "Now you know the necessity that I had mentioned to you concerning this journey. For you share the root of their souls." And he told them their names and their fathers' names and where they were from. Then the sage asked, "What was their iniquity? The Rabbi answered, "They are being punished for the iniquity of shaving the corners of their heads." "And what connection is there between marring the corners of one's beard and oxen?" The Ari said to him, "Did you not encounter this in your studies?"

"My master, this thing is written neither in the Gemara[5] nor in the Midrash."[6]

"It is written explicitly in the Bible."

"There is no such verse in the Torah."

The Ari explained: "It is written, 'You shall not shave the corners of your head and you shall not destroy . . .'[7] The initials of those words make up the word *PaROT*[8] (cows), indicating that all those who round off or destroy the corners of the face or the beard transmigrate into cows. You must work to repair their condition. So fast tomorrow, and cultivate the proper inner intent with those particular persons in mind."

And he wrote for him all the acts of penance and the ascetic practices that he had to fulfill in order to attain *tikkun* for the souls of those men.

And they appeared to the sage in a dream and said to him, "May the Lord bless you. May your mind know rest just as our souls found rest from the very day that you commenced to perform the acts of penance that the Rabbi indicated to you. For with the very first acts of penance on your part we were brought out from the difficult labor that you saw and were allowed to enter into Gehenna.[9] Similarly, with every further act of penance that you performed, we were brought out from a heavier to a lighter yoke until we were brought into our own place."[10]

Ḥemdat yamim, Shabbat 19b–20a

1. A rabbi in Damascus during the sixteenth and early seventeenth centuries, remembered primarily as a legal scholar. Gershom Scholem (*Beḥinot bevikoret uvesifrut* 8 [1955]: 84) points out that this legend, found earlier in *Sefer maasei nissim,* makes of Abulafia, who had cast serious doubt on the Ari's miracles, a participant in one of the latter's wondrous episodes.
2. Literally "did not know where there is light."
3. Deuteronomy 32:36.
4. See the Introduction.
5. The vaster portions of both the Babylonian and Palestinian Talmuds, which consist of discussions on the Mishnah.
6. A body of exegetical literature on the biblical text.
7. Leviticus 19:27.
8. The word consists of the first letters of the words, *peat rashekhem velo tashḥit,* the *vav* read also as a letter that can signify the vowel sound *o* (*ḥolem*). This connection between shaving and cows is found also in Nathan ben Reuben David Spiro, *Maamar yayin hameshumar* (Venice, 1660). See Meir Benayahu, *Sefer toledot haari* (Jerusalem, 1967), 114.
9. Hell.
10. Or, "our present place." The same basic story is found in the collections of the Ari legends (See Benayahu, *Sefer toledot haari,* p. 114).

Aspects of this legend recall at least two stories associated directly or indirectly with the Ashkenazic pietism of the twelfth and thirteenth centuries. This movement clearly influenced the value system and ethical literature of sixteenth-century Safed. One story, found in Moses Gaster's, *Maaseh Buch* (vol. 2 [Philadelphia, 1934], no. 170, p. 353) and quoted immediately following our legend in the text of

Ḥemdat yamim, relates to Rabbi Judah the Hasid, the foremost figure of the earlier Ashkenazic pietism. It concerns the very same subject: severe punishment, or the threat of such, to be inflicted following death on one who cut off the corners of his beard. In that legend, Rabbi Judah warns the transgressor, a wealthy man, that if he fails to heed his warning concerning shaving his beard with a razor, demons in the form of large cows will come and trample him. After the man's death, a demon in the form of a cow placed the man's soul in a container filled with brimstone and pitch. That legend similarly explains that the initial letters of the prohibition in Leviticus 19:27 form the word *PaROT* (cows).

Although it does not refer to rounding the corners of one's head or marring one's beard, another story, found in *Sefer ḥasidim* (MS Bologna, no. 169; MS Parma, no. 63) and also in *Maaseh Buch* (vol. 2, p. 654, no. 251), contains a more striking series of similarities to the legend of Rabbi Jacob Abulafia. A person finds himself alone in a desert and discovers human beings, no longer alive, pulling one another in carts. They exchange places and continue to pull one another, thus performing a function normally assigned to animals— as their punishment for various sins they had committed during their lifetimes. These were sins that reduced them to the moral equivalent of animals; or they were acts of mistreatment of animals. As with the preceding legend, this one too includes both punishment after death and a disclosure of that punishment and its causes to the living. It would appear that shaving the corners of one's beard, considered a very grave offense, merged with an earlier narrative tradition of this type.

Various features of these narratives are echoed in the later legend of the Ari and Rabbi Jacob Abulafia. But the latter story assimilates the motif of the Ari's wondrous knowledge as the broader framework into which the other elements in the legend are fitted. In addition, the reader overhears in the later story overtones both of the concept of *gilgul* (metempsychosis) as a man becomes an ox, and, more to the point, of *tikkun* and the need to repair the effects of the misdeed. *Tikkun* goes beyond the mere request and granting of forgiveness as found in the legend of Rabbi Judah the Hasid. In the story, it is the Ari (in whose world outlook *tikkun* historically comprised a fundamental pillar) who knows the way of *tikkun* for any particular person and situation.

This legend exemplifies a basic polarity of rest and unrest in moving from the antithesis of rest, a situation of painful affliction for the dead souls undergoing punishment, to the rest that comes through Abulafia's acts of *tikkun*. And moreover, the same polarity of rest and torment reverberates also in the personal experience of Rabbi Abulafia. Together with the other members of the caravan, he rests, presumably in the heat of the day. His rest, in particular, is intensified in the form of a deep sleep, only to be followed by a tormenting experience that allows him no rest. In fact, it is his very resting that brings him to the state of unrest and fright. Later, upon returning to the caravan, he finds relief following the tormenting sight he had witnessed. Furthermore, the terrifying unrest experienced by Abulafia is a necessary component of the process of bringing the afflicted men to a condition of rest.

The motif of rest is subtly reinforced by a series of richly connotative, interrelated terms drawn from the biblical tradition: Egypt, the desert, and *menuhah* (rest). Following their Egyptian servitude and wilderness wanderings, the Israelites found *menuhah venahalah* (rest and an inheritance). This pattern of associations is further intensified by the phrase, *hotsiyanu meotah haavodah hakashah* (they brought us forth from that difficult labor), which is basic to the biblical account of the Exodus (Exodus 1:14; 3:10; 6:9; 7:5; 12:51; 13:14; 13:16; 26:6).

The pattern of the first discussion between Rabbi Abulafia and the Ari is repeated in their second discussion. In each case the Ari, without being told, knows and explains why his guest has come to him. The Rabbi's wondrous knowledge, conveyed by his information that the journey is "of great necessity" (without spelling out the nature of that necessity) is echoed later in his knowing both the reason for the affliction of the two men and the appropriate *tikkunim* for liberating them from their torment. In this respect, the Ari is the central figure in the story, the agent who brings the transgressors to a state of rest. Rabbi Abulafia, then, serves merely as a subagent who carries out the directives of the Ari. Although he has his own reasons for going to Egypt, on another level he is going as his master's agent—in ways and for reasons he himself does not at all comprehend.

The same story, however, lends itself to another reading, one in which Rabbi Abulafia is the central figure. He is told that he shares the root of the souls of the two afflicted men, a piece of information that can unlock the meaning of the story as a whole. Implied, then, is that he himself requires *tikkun*—because of the soul-root shared in common—and can attain such inner purification only through leading the two afflicted men to *tikkun*. Thus not only the two men but also Rabbi Abulafia attains his *tikkun*, his state of greater wholeness and, hence, of rest.

If so, it follows that the pupil's desire to journey to Egypt was really a sign of his inner unrest, his lack of wholeness. He was driven to go in order to repair the root of his soul and that of his partners, even though, given the limitations of his powers of self-perception, he looked upon the journey as one of his own choice for his own conscious purposes. This concept of the shared root-soul adds additional meanings to the rest-unrest polarity in the legend and also deepens the irony in Abulafia's request to make his journey.

This legend exemplifies a motif common to many of the Ari legends: A character acts on the basis of certain choices that he believes to be his own, but the Ari perceives those same acts and choices in terms of a larger pattern that others do not grasp. The Ari's insight affirms a deeper understanding of events: Nothing is coincidental or self-explanatory; meaning transcends appearances.

Deed and Consequence

Reward and Punishment
of a Corpse

I

The quality of silence brings blessedness in the
world to come.

The Ḥasid Rabbi Lepidot—may he rest in peace—testified to my
teacher[1]—may he rest in peace—that in a dream he saw the wise Ḥasid
Rabbi Judah ben Shoshan—may he rest in peace—after the latter's
death here in the Upper Galilee. And he noted that his face was radiant
like the light of the sun, with each and every hair of his beard iridescent
like a torch. When asked how he merited this, he answered that it was
due to his quality of silence, for in all his years he never participated
in frivolous chatter.

Reshit ḥokhmah, Shaar haahavah 6

    1. Rabbi Moses Cordovero (1522–1570).

II

A corpse reveals punishment of the individual
after death and burial.

In our time, in the kingdom of Fez,[1] it happened that a Ḥasid died
away from his land in a village a day's distance from his home, and
there he was buried. Some years later when the sons of that Ḥasid
went to bring his remains to be interred with members of his family,
they found that except for one leg his body had not decomposed. This
fact saddened his oldest son, for he thought, why had that one leg
decomposed? Perhaps worms and maggots will continue to consume
him.

    The father then appeared to the son in a dream and told him,
"Know that worms have not consumed me except for that one leg,
which once kicked a master of Torah. But the rest of my body, which

did not share in the sin against him, has remained whole and will continue to remain secure from the ravage of worms.

I have heard this from a wise old man who had heard it, in turn, from the son of that Ḥasid, and the son is still alive.

Reshit ḥokhmah, Shaar haahavah 6

1. In Morocco.

The Father Who Would Not Reprimand His Son

A father's refusal to reprimand his son's irreverence brings on tragic consequences.

A man was standing in the synagogue with his son, and while all the people were responding, "Hallelujah,"[1] following the chanting of the words, his son answered with words of foolishness.

People said to the father, "Look at your son who responds with foolishness." But he answered, "What can I do with him? He is a young child who is playful by nature." Again the following day the son did the same thing and similarly all eight days of the festival,[2] while his father said nothing to him.

Not a year passed without a death in the family. The man died and also his wife and his son and grandson. A total of fifteen died in his family. The one surviving couple consisted of one who was lame and blind and one who was an idiot and wicked.[3]

Reshit ḥokhmah, Shaar hayirah 4

1. "Praise the Lord," the phrase concluding many of the psalms of the Hallel (Psalms 113–118).
2. The seven days of the Sukkot festival and the additional day of Shemini Atzeret (the Eighth Day of Assembly).
3. Note the rhythm of the tale with its abrupt ending on a note of baffling catastrophe that, within a brief period of time, completely devastates the family. This account is found also in *Ḥemdat yamim* (1763) *Rosh ḥodesh* 32a.

The Reward for Hospitality

A brilliant son is born to a childless couple as the reward for their hospitality to Jews in flight.

Jehiel[1] was an elderly man who resided in a city along the Mediterranean coast at the time of the decrees of expulsion from Spain and Portugal. At the time of the decrees in those lands, when many Jews were fleeing to Turkey, this man of unblemished integrity would receive the poor and the wealthy alike with a cheerful countenance. He would provide them with bread and water and food and also accompany them on their way and give them provision for the journey. He expended much money to meet the needs of his guests.

Once four elderly Jews, great sages—all of them from the lands of the exile—were at his house. And when they saw his wealth and his great glory—for he contributed from his heart and lovingly assisted both rich and poor on their way to exile—the four elders asked him, "What is your request from the Creator, may He be blessed?

He responded that he does have a request, namely, that he might be given a son, for he was childless. The four elders told him, "Know for a certainty that within a year you will have a son, one who will be renowned in Torah. And you shall name him Abraham as a sign that you practiced loving-kindness toward the seed of Abraham."[2]

And just as they had promised, so it was that a son, the brilliant rabbi Rabbenu Abraham da Pisa, was born to him, a son who attained great heights in Torah and who composed many books.[3]

Kav hayashar 18:13–14

1. Several members of the da Pisa family, among the wealthiest of Jewish bankers in Italy, were noted for their assistance and hospitality to Jews visiting from other lands (Cecil Roth, *History of the Jews of Italy* [Philadelphia, 1946], 179, 192). This was particularly true of Isaac ben Vitale (Jehiel), who assisted refugees on their way to Turkey following their expulsion from Spain and Portugal.

2. More likely, the name Abraham is designated to signify the father's fulfilling the quality of hospitality that characterizes the patriarch Abraham in both biblical and midrashic tradition.

3. While Isaac's son Daniel was noted for preparing a code of law for the Jewish community of Rome, the much more noted scholar and author in the family was Isaac's nephew Vitale (Jehiel) Nissim ben Simone da Pisa, author of *Minḥat kenaot*

(ms. Mantua, 1559, published by David Kaufman, [Berlin, 1898]), a comparison of religion and philosophy, and of *Maamar hayyei olam* (1962, Gilbert Rosenthal, *Banking and Finance Among Jews in Renaissance Italy* [New York, 1962]), a treatise on banking in Jewish law. Presumably Isaac and Vitale, uncle and nephew, are the historical figures behind the legend.

The pattern in this account mirrors that of Genesis 18 (see n. 2) in which Abraham, who displays hospitality toward travelers in the desert, is told that his wife Sarah will give birth to a son even at her advanced age. In a later legend relating to the birth of the Baal Shem Tov, his father, Eliezer, shows hospitality to Elijah, who appears as a stranger coming on the Sabbath. Elijah then announces to his host the coming birth of a son of outstanding significance (*Maasiyot umaamarim yekarim* [Zhitomir, 1902], 2). Note also the story of the son of a hospitable man found in Joseph S. Farhi, *Oseh peleh* (Berlin, vol. 3 1902), 72–76, translated in part in *Memekor yisrael* (Bloomington, 1976), 1052–1056.

Najara and the Vanishing and Returning Angels

Because of his wondrous knowledge, the Ari notes events hidden from human eyes and interprets them as the consequence of a lack of reverence.

In the days of the wondrous light, the Ari—may his memory be for a blessing for the life of the world to come—there lived the sage Israel Najara—[1]may he rest in peace—who was a sweet psalmist of Israel.[2] It happened once on the night of the holy Sabbath, while that wise man was singing at his table as was his good custom, that the Rabbi— may his memory be for a blessing—saw hosts of angels in motion[3] coming to Najara's house to delight in his songs. And immediately the Rabbi saw that one angel appeared and drove away the entire camp of angels present there because Najara's arms were uncovered and because there was no covering upon his head while he was seated at the table in the presence of the Lord.[4]

When the Rabbi sensed the matter, he sent for our teachers Rabbi Hayyim Vital[5] and Rabbi Y. Ha-Kohen to disclose the secret to Najara, informing him that heavenly angels had been there taking delight with him at his table but had departed because he had no sense of fear and awe in the Lord's presence. Now when that wise man, Israel, heard the words of the Rabbi's students, trembling took hold of him and he stood shaking. And he sat with great reverence, wrapped in his cloak with a covering upon his head, and resumed his singing, this time with both joy and trembling. Immediately the angels of God were again ascending and descending there[6] as at the beginning, glad and rejoicing as in wedding dances . . .

Ḥemdat yamim, Shabbat 55b

1. Israel Najara, who lived from the mid-sixteenth through the first quarter of the seventeenth century, was the outstanding Hebrew poet of his time. His poetic activity and his prominence can both be dated considerably after the Ari's death, but the legend freely recreates historical chronology in making the two figures contemporaries. Almost the entirety of Najara's prolific output revolves around the themes of exile and redemption, and in time his poems spread to many Jewish communities.
2. Samuel 23:1.
3. Psalms 68:16, which gives a sense of fleeing.

4. Ezekiel 41:22.
5. Student of the Ari and author of *Ets ḥayyim,* in which he sets forth his master's teachings.
6. Genesis 28:12.

This legend appears also in the collections of the Ari legends (see Meir Benayahu, *Sefer toledot haari* [Jerusalem, 1967], 230–231).

At the beginning of this legend, Najara displays joy devoid of trembling, that is, lacking in spiritual gravity. In the world of Safed Kabbalah, joy is a definite religious value—especially when associated with the Sabbath, which, in the text of the legend, connotes a wedding. It must be combined, however, with the graver emotions also associated with religious life, for by itself it can easily deteriorate into light-headedness and levity. The legend suggests that when the necessary qualities of trembling and awe are lacking, they nonetheless became present in appalling ways. At the end of the legend the danger is averted as the poet's mood combines both joy and trembling.

The wider context in *Ḥemdat yamim* emphasizes the importance of dress: The combination of joy and trembling is expressed in one's being clad in white garments, which recall the angels. A similar emphasis is found in that text in the discussion of the penitential prayers preceding the Days of Awe—the act of prayer at that time requires proper clothing and the covering of both head and body (*Ḥemdat yamim* [1763] *Yamim noraim* 12b). Even though one's prayer and song might in themselves be pleasing to God, they are not desirable in His eyes and are even likened to idolatry if they occur in a setting of disrespectful dress (*Ḥemdat yamim* [1763], *Yamim noraim* 13a).

This legend, in its combination of praise and criticism of Najara, appears to reflect an ambivalence on the part of the pietistic Kabbalists toward the poet. Although his poetry is deeply religious in its themes, it borrows popular melodies and poetic modes from the Arabs of the Near East, melodies and poetic qualities drawn, in this case, from a milieu believed to be remote from the piety and spirituality of the mystics of Safed in particular (Solomon Rozanes, *Korot hayehudim beturkiah veartsot hakedem,* vol. 3 [Sofia, 1938], 222). Najara's association with Arabic poets and musicians led him to the life of physical delights that characterized the world of Arab poets (Rozanes, *Korot hayehudim,* p. 223), delights that had no place in the life of the sixteenth-century Kabbalists and their successors.

This gave rise, in turn, to accusations of virtually every kind of immorality. Najara is accused of drunkenness (sources quoted in Rozanes, *Korot hayehudim*, p. 223), a charge that accompanies the accusation that he opens poems with Hebrew words resembling Arabic words that speak of a case of adultery. Hayyim Vital mentions that he has been told concerning Najara that the poet was not worthy of being included in a group of Damascus scholars called together for the purpose of repentance (*Sefer hahezionot*, ed. Aharon Z. Eshkoli [Jerusalem, 1954], 23). And although he praises the poems, Vital declared it forbidden for anyone to read them aloud, charging the poet with lewd speech, drunkenness, expelling his wife from his house so that he could have intimate relations with a strange woman, and engaging in homosexual acts while in an intoxicated state (*Sefer hahezionot*, p. 34). More pertinent to the legend, Vital charged that once, while in Egypt, Najara placed his hat on the ground during a meal and then sang in a loud voice, while eating meat and drinking wine to excess (*Sefer hahezionot*, p. 34). What these accusations probably indicate, apart from the moral degeneracy some attribute to the poet's cultural borrowings, is Najara's talents both in writing poetry and in making enemies.

The version of this same legend in another part of *Hemdat yamim* ([1763] *Yamim noraim* 12b) refers to Najara as "a spark of King David," an expression that gives a distinct Sabbatean stamp to the legend. Gershom Scholem ("Shir shel yisrael najara befi hashabtaim," in *Ignace Goldziher Memorial Volume*, vol. 1, ed. Samuel Löwinger and Joseph Somogyi [Budapest, 1948], 41–44) pointed out that this description of Najara that appears in the name of the Ari is not found in any of the earlier sources. That description is found, however, in Sabbatean references to the poet (Scholem, "Shir shel yisrael najara, p. 41 n.1), and the Sabbateans interpreted his poems relating to redemption as prophecies of the coming of Sabbatai Zevi, the seventeenth-century heretical messiah.

The Importance
of Precision

*Wages paid to a worker must be precise and
meticulously fair.*

In the days of the Rabbi (the Ari)—may his memory be for a blessing—
Rabbi A. Galanti[1] requested of him to repair his soul. The Rabbi then
trembled greatly due to his colleague's exalted position until Galanti
warned him, "If you do not tell me all that you perceive in my forehead,[2] I will require that you take an oath to tell me," and then the
Ari proceeded to read his forehead.

He said to him, "There is a possibility of theft concerning my
master and teacher." The rabbi thereupon gave a profound shudder
and said, "How can I bear that shame of the iniquity of theft?" Sullen
and depressed, he went home and clad himself in sackcloth and ashes.
And he called together the workers who made clothing in his employ.
They came to him, and, finding the rabbi clad in sackcloth and sitting
upon the ground, they were alarmed, all of them. The rabbi said to
them, "Do you know, do you not hear that I am flesh and blood and
I do not desire to enter Gehenna[3] as a result of unclean hands; therefore
if from this moment on you are meticulous in calculating the wages of
your work, then it will be well, but if not, then leave me."

They answered him, "How can we go about figuring out our
wages, for from the day we began working for you we have lacked
nothing; nor shall we be in need, for blessing rests upon us and we
have more than enough to eat. There is none among us willing to make
an accounting of your money." Then the rabbi said to them, "Surely
the matter is known, and the reason I have stumbled into the iniquity
of theft is that you do not keep a strict accounting of what I owe you.
Therefore I will now place money before you that each may take what
you desire, and you will forgive me for whatever I might have in my
possession that is rightfully yours, and also I will forgive you. He placed
money before them, but they refused to take even the smallest coin
except for one woman who took two such coins, and they all answered
as one, saying, "We have forgiven you completely, down to the last
coin, and so on."

The rabbi rose and went to the academy of the Rabbi—may his
memory be for a blessing for the life of the world to come—who had

already gone forth to greet him and who said to Galanti, "What is all this trembling on your part, my master?" He answered, "Is it a light matter to be guilty of possible theft? If I have found favor in your eyes, discern, please, and look upon my forehead to note if anything remains of the guilt."

The Rabbi answered, "There is no iniquity of yours here," and he disclosed to Galanti the secret concerning that possibility of theft, telling him that it had to do with that very woman who reached out for the two coins. That woman weaved with a most delicate skill beyond that of the other weavers, and so she had deserved to receive more but had, in fact, received earnings equal to those of the other artisans. And concerning this matter they are very exacting with my master in the upper worlds, and he showed him the imprint in writing upon his forehead.

Ḥemdat yamim, Yamim noraim 53ab

1. A follower of Rabbi Moses Cordovero (1522–1570) and author of *Zohare ḥammah* (Venice, 1655).
2. An aspect of the dimensions of wondrous knowledge of the Ari. It is reported in the name of the Ari that "all the mitzvot and the transgressions that a person does are recognizable on his forehead" (*Shulḥan arukh shel haari, Keviut hatorah* 15). The Zohar (2:76a) speaks of the belief that hidden facts of one's personality can be read from the lines of hands and fingers. The Ari, however, focused solely on the forehead. See Lawrence Fine, "The Art of Metoposcopy: A Study in Isaac Luria's Charismatic Knowledge," *AJS Review* 11 (1986), 79–102.
3. Hell.

The financial "misdemeanor" involved only two small coins, a measure of the degree of exactness demanded and a reflection of the overall belief that any act, regardless of how insignificant it might appear on the surface, is of great importance.

In this story, the workers, in their trust of Galanti, brought him to the brink of guilt. The act of repair required him to resist precisely that sense of trust on their part: Their lack of exactness in figuring their earnings from him is pitted against a divine exactness.

On the weaving craft in Safed and its economic importance during the sixteenth century, see Shmuel Avitsur, "Safed: Center for Textile Weaving in the Sixteenth Century" (in Hebrew) *Sefunot 6* (1962): 41–69.

Repentance and Penance

The Anonymous Penitent

The virtue of anonymity in repentance.

In the days of the Ari—may his memory be for a blessing for the life of the world to come—there was one man, a penitent, who from time to time would go to the synagogue after midnight clad from head to toe in sackcloth so that people might not recognize him. And he would turn his face toward the wall,[1] standing there half the night[2] and all the following day until midnight, praying, pleading, and weeping. Only after midnight when everyone was asleep would he leave the synagogue to go home, and absolutely no one knew who he was.

The Rabbi (the Ari) used to say that this certainly exemplifies complete and perfect repentance.[3] For repentance and almsgiving are on the same level: Just as almsgiving is most perfect when done in secret, so is repentance when it is done in a clandestine manner. And such secrecy is beneficial in that the other side[4] is unable to prevail over the penitent to make him depart from the ways of repentance.

Ḥemdat yamim, Yamim noraim 48b

1. It is appropriate for a penitent to rise at night to weep because of his former sins (*Reshit ḥokhmah, Shaar hakedushah* 7).
2. A person praying should stand next to the wall with nothing between himself and the wall (Zohar 1:228a).
3. *Ḥemdat yamim* quotes a passage from *Sefer ḥasidim* (MS. Bologne, no. 8) prescribing that a person's repentance be done secretly, so that "his heart find no enjoyment in his good deeds."
4. *Sitra aḥera*, the world of demonic forces.

The complete anonymity of the penitent lends a mysterious nuance to the account. His penance, hidden from society's eyes, takes place purely between man and God in a purity of motivation. It shares this quality with the hidden righteous of later stories, whose true identity and character are, similarly, concealed from the eyes of humanity. Symbolizing the penance-oriented spirituality of the world of Lurianic Kabbalah, the anonymous figure in the tale exemplifies an impressive strength of will.

This same account is found almost word-for-word in *Kav hayashar* 48:6. There, however, it acquires a narrative context as it follows the account of Rabbi Abraham ben Eliezer ha-Levi Berukhim, who gathered together Jews in order to awaken them to repentance by having them submit themselves symbolically to the four kinds of death sentences mentioned in the talmudic legal sources. Within that broader context, the author of *Kav hayashar* recounts the case of this one penitent whose penitence was done in complete secrecy and anonymity. Lifted out of that narrative context and standing alone as it appears here in *Ḥemdat yamim,* the anecdote acquires an even more dramatic quality.

The Ari and the Penitent

A man guilty of a grave sin is prepared to die as
his way of atonement. His very readiness to die
atones for his past.

In the days of the Rabbi (the Ari)—may his memory be for a blessing
for the life of the world to come—it happened that a rich person came
to him with the purpose of testing his knowledge. The Rabbi told him
that he had seven abominations in his heart and disclosed to him all
the details of the transgressions that he had committed. The Rabbi also
told the wealthy man that he had had sexual relations with his maid.
The man acknowledged all his transgressions without embarrassment,
denying only his having had intimate relations with his maid. This he
would not acknowledge until the Rabbi told him, "Now you will see
me produce that accursed one in your presence." And the Rabbi placed
his hands upon that man and produced the maid's image and likeness,
a harlot and a scoundrel, and the man recognized her and declared,
"She is more righteous than I."

His soul almost departed as he fell at the Rabbi's feet saying, "I
have sinned and have clearly transgressed." And the Rabbi—may he
rest in peace—restored his soul to him. Then the man cried with a
bitter voice, crying and pleading before the Rabbi, "Just remove this
death from me!" He answered, "This is yours in order that you will
know that the sages said in truth that one who has [illicit] intimate
relations with a non-Jewish woman will be bound with her like a dog
even in the world to come.[1] She is bound to you and will depart only
with great repentance and acts of rectification." The man responded,
"Behold, I am prepared to accept even the four deaths imposed by the
court."[2] Then the Rabbi answered him, "Your penance is through
burning."

As the man heard this, he took out money from his pocket to
purchase wood with which to burn himself. The Rabbi told him that
his judgment was not like that of the other nations, for according to
Jewish law it was necessary to throw a boiling lead wick into the
mouth.[3] And the man answered, "Whatever happens, I shall die." The
Rabbi then ordered that lead be purchased, and they brought it and
placed it upon the fire. The Rabbi told him to recite the confession
[*viddui*] of one dangerously ill. And he did so.

He told him, "Throw yourself to the ground." And he lay down on the ground. He said to him, "Stretch out your hands." And he stretched them out. "Close your eyes." And he closed them. "Open your mouth." And he opened it. The Rabbi immediately threw into his mouth various kinds of sweets that he had on hand for the occasion and said to him, "Your iniquity is removed and your sin is atoned. The Lord has removed your sin. You shall not die."

And the Rabbi raised him from the ground and wrote for him acts of *tikkun* for his soul. As part of the acts of penance he commanded him to read each day five pages from the Zohar, even though the man told him that the Lord had withheld this wisdom from him and that he was totally unfamiliar with it. Nevertheless he commanded him to read, even without understanding, in order to mend his soul.

And that man died in a state of complete repentance.[4]

Ḥemdat yamim, Yamim noraim 5b–6a

1. Sota 3b, mentioned also in *Reshit ḥokhmah, Shaar hayirah* 8.
2. Mishnah Sanhedrin 7:1.
3. Ibid. 7:2.
4. Background and commentary on this legend follow the next story, "Moses de Leon and the Penitent," to which it is closely related.

Moses de Leon
and the Penitent

Another version of the same legend.

In a mood of jest, a man who had lived a completely wicked life and who knew that only with the greatest difficulty might his repentance be accepted once asked Rabbi M. de Leon[1]—may his memory be for a blessing—if there could be any healing for his transgressions. The sage told him that he had no possibility of healing or atoning for his iniquities. The man then asked him whether, if he accepted the sentence of death, he would have a portion in Paradise. The rabbi told him, "Yes." The man answered, "Swear to me that my place there will be near yours," and the rabbi swore to him that he would attempt to draw the man near to himself in Paradise.

The man followed the master to his house of study where the sage, Rabbi M. de Leon, commanded that lead be brought to him, and lead was brought to him. He prepared the lead until it was well beaten. And afterward he seated the man upon a small bench and took a small scarf, which he tied over his eyes. He said to the man, "Confess to our God concerning all your iniquities, accept the yoke of God's Kingdom wholeheartedly, and say *Shema yisrael*,[2] and accept death in exchange for your iniquities with which you angered your Creator all your days." And the penitent did all that the rabbi commanded him and wept profusely and bitterly while a large group of elders and scholars stood around him.

Afterward the rabbi said to him, "Open your mouth and I will throw a lead wick into it." And the man opened his mouth as wide as he could while all those around him beheld this with their own eyes. Then the rabbi took a large spoonful of rose honey, poured it into his mouth, and said to him, "Your iniquity is removed and your sin is atoned."

The penitent immediately began to cry out in a voice of bitterness, "My master, for the sake of God, please kill me so that I will not have to witness the loss of my soul. Why should I desire life, given my very many iniquities?" But the rabbi told him, "Have no fear, and do not be dismayed, for God has already accepted your deeds."[3] And ever since that time, the penitent did not depart from the master's house of

115

study, where he devoted all his days to fasting and to great repentance; and words of study did not cease to flow from his mouth.

Following these things, the rabbi was called to the heavenly academy, dying and departing for his eternal home. And when that penitent saw that his master had died, he cried with bitterness of soul and prayed to God—may He be blessed—to take him too, since he was left without a rabbi to guide him. He prayed with such fervor that God hearkened to his voice and the man became ill. And as he approached death, he began to shout, "Make room for our rabbi and teacher, M. de Leon, for he is coming for me now to fulfill his oath to bring me near to him in Paradise."

Immediately afterward the man died, and following his death some elders and great ones saw him in a dream sitting in Paradise alongside his master as they studied Torah together.

Or hayashar, Amud gemilut hasadim (Amsterdam, 1709, 40b)

1. Moses de Leon (d. 1305), thirteenth-century Spanish Jewish mystic, considered by modern scholarship to be the author of the Zohar.
2. The affirmation of God's Oneness, Deuteronomy 6:4.
3. Ecclesiastes 9:7.

The account of a repentant sinner who is willing and even anxious to undergo death as a prescribed path of atonement is found in various texts of the Ari legends. Examination of these sources suggests certain layers of development both of the basic story line and of the literary rendering of the legends.

A story included in *Sefer hakavanot umaaseh nissim* (Constantinople, 1720) appears to contain the nucleus of this legend-tradition (6ab). We read there that a rich man from Constantinople, credited with a vast repertoire of transgressions, set out for Safed with the intention of repenting, but only on condition that the Ari disclose to him all his sins. While the man stopped at an inn during the course of his journey, the Ari, who disclosed to his students the stranger's imminent arrival in Safed and his purpose in testing him, related also that this stranger bears the soul of the wicked biblical king, Ahab. Upon arriving in Safed and meeting with the Ari, the rich man is struck with terror as the rabbi discloses to him in detail all his sins and deeds. The rich man admits to his sins and declares his willingness to repent. The sage then prescribes for him the relevant *tikkun,* the particular procedure for rectifying his transgressions and their spiritual effect. And the former sinner, who then sent for his wife and children, later died in Safed in a state of complete repentance.

The various versions of the collection *Sefer toledot haari* (ed. Meir Benayahu [Jerusalem, 1967], 173–174) include a telling of the same basic legend while adding at least one significant element. There, a wealthy man from Constantinople came to celebrate the Passover festival in Safed, where he heard of the Ari's wondrous knowledge, specifically his ability to reveal even to a complete stranger all his transgressions, including details of time and place. The visitor returned to Constantinople and told of the sage's wondrous cognitive abilities to a fellow townsman, one said to be guilty of every possible transgression. The latter decided to travel to Safed in order to test the Ari: If the sage indeed disclosed to him all his iniquities, he would repent; and if not, then, as in the previous legend, he would know that the world functions in disregard of moral or religious considerations. As in the previous legend from *Sefer hakavanot umaaseh nissim,* the Ari's supernatural knowledge is displayed in his knowing and revealing what had occurred even at great distance, prior to the man's reaching Safed.

When the stranger arrived in Safed, the Ari disclosed to him his name along with all his transgressions, including their time and place. The visitor consequently confessed and requested the necessary *tikkun* to mend his soul of the effects of his wrongdoings. He went on to swear, "If you tell me that I can have no *tikkun* except through death or strangling I will agree to these in order to atone for my iniquities"—an utterance not found in the previous telling of the legend. In fact, the Ari prescribed for him various other procedures to mend his soul and, as in the previous telling of the legend, the former sinner attains to a state of perfect and complete repentance.

Although both narrations concern repentance, the legends place their fundamental emphasis upon the wondrous knowledge of the Ari, which extends even to the secret deeds of people whom he has never previously met. The statement of the repentant sinner expressing his desire for atone for his sins even should such atonement require his death foreshadows the direction that this legend took in other tellings, marked by a radicalization of the narrative line.

A degree of such radicalization is readily evident in another form of the legend included in *Shivḥei haari,* Meir Benayahu, *Sefer toledot haari* (Jerusalem, 1967), 238–239. Without indicating the place of residence of the rich man, the legend begins by repeating the general lines of the story as we have come to recognize them. Then the rich man admits to all the transgressions the Ari revealed to him except to one, which he vehemently denies, namely, his having had sexual relations with a maidservant. The Ari, however, responds to that denial by reproducing for the stranger the likeness of the maidservant, a likeness that is now physically bound to him. The man almost dies from shock and requests that the Ari remove the likeness of the maidservant from him. But, he is told, that requires complete repentance and numerous acts of penance. The man replies, "Let him do with me whatever is necessary, even to the extent of the four kinds of death imposed by the court," and he states his willingness to die even a thousand deaths, if that is what is called for.

The Ari informs him that his particular sin requires death by burning and proceeds to send for molten lead to be placed in the man's throat. The text then continues along the lines of the text found in *Ḥemdat yamim*. Unlike the first two legends discussed above, the episode during the journey to Safed is missing, and one might speculate that this is because the Ari's wondrous knowledge—the subject of an episode set either at an inn or alongside a river—is no longer the major thrust of the legend as it appears here. True, the legend attributes to the Ari, in addition to his wondrous knowledge, both the ability to reproduce the likeness of the maidservant (an act so startling that it pierces the armor of the rich man) and the ability to announce that God has accepted his repentance. The major thrust of the legend, however, is the extent of the will to repent; and the central figure is no longer the Ari but rather the former sinner who becomes a wholehearted penitent.

The statement of a willingness to die if necessary in order to atone for one's sins is transformed into action as the man demonstrates his readiness to die and, indeed, actually believes himself to be dying as his way of penance. Thus a legend rooted in the intent to extol the Ari and his wondrous knowledge developed in directions going far beyond that original intent.

The basic elements of this legend, with only slight variation, are found also in another tale of the Ari included in *Sefer hakavanot umaaseh nissim* 6a, appearing there immediately following the very first legend discussed in this analysis. There are other examples as well of tales representing different levels of development of the same basic legend-tradition being preserved in the same literary source.

For this reason, in part, the dates of the literary collections themselves do not serve as a basis for a reconstruction of the legend-tradition.

The version of this legend translated from *Hemdat yamim* for this collection is carefully constructed in terms of a tension between seeking and avoiding death. First, the man sought to avoid the "death" present in the trauma of beholding the likeness of the maidservant that the Ari brought into being. Then, however, upon learning of his punishment extending to the world to come, he begged to die in order to atone for his sin. He went through the motions of dying by fire thinking that he was, in fact, dying—with the result that he was saved from death. And in the conclusion, as in the other legends of this type, we are told that he died in a state of complete repentance.

The second version of this same basic legend, translated in our collection (and found also in *Hemdat yamim* [1763] *Yamim noraim* 27a), relates to Rabbi Moses de Leon. While all the various tellings of this legend-tradition concern the relationship between a sinner or former sinner and a sage, this legend accentuates that relationship and places it at the thematic center of the story. In this account—unlike in the previous texts of this legend-tradition—the change in the sinner is not dependent upon any disclosure of his secret sin by the wise man. The man made no effort to conceal his wrongdoings from the rabbi. Not the wondrous knowledge of the master but the promise of the eternal presence of the sage in Paradise prompted the metamorphosis of the sinner into the penitent. It is the sinner's attraction to the sage that overcame his evil propensities: Only the promise of the sage's eternal presence made him willing, even determined, to die for the sake of atonement.

Later, the penitent's activity in Paradise—studying with his teacher—as perceived in the dream of the living is but a continuation, beyond the grave, of his adopted and chosen course in life. There is, however, an additional nuance in that the two are studying together (*beyahad*). The word connotes a sense of equality of status between the sage and the truly repentant sinner, one making for a true togetherness and suggesting the man's complete liberation from the imprint and impact of his negative past.

Comparing this legend of Moses de Leon with the various versions of the same legend-tradition that relate to the Ari, one notes that the tradition has been completely disassociated from the motif of wondrous knowledge. And one might suggest that the legend's outgrowing the motif of wondrous knowledge, so central to the Ari legends, is responsible for the choice of another personage as the rabbi in the legend, a figure not marked by that strong association with the motif.

This legend-tradition clearly stemmed from a body of teaching going back to a talmudic statement (Yoma 86a; note also Genesis Rabba 65:22) that there are sins for which one can atone only by death. The literature of the period explains the practice of flagellation (*malkut*) preceding Yom Kippur as the acceptance of an affliction symbolizing the types of death that, in antiquity, the rabbinical court had been empowered to decree (*Ḥemdat yamim* [1763] *Yamim noraim* 5b–6a).

In other ways, too, pious Jews, particularly in Safed, afflicted themselves in various ways designed to represent those four kinds of death (*Ḥemdat yamim* [1763] *Rosh ḥodesh* 4a; *Kav hayashar*, chapter 48 [1873], 414–415; Benayahu, *Sefer toledot haari*, 226–227). Similarly both sacrifices and their substitute, prayer, were interpreted as the penitent's undergoing a symbolic death in place of a supposedly deserved physical death (*Kav hayashar* 59:5). The reciting of the statements accompanying the *nefilat apayim* (prostration or kneeling to the full extent of placing one's head on the ground following prayer) is said to suggest the worshiper's surrendering to death with the actual intent to die and offer his soul to the Shekhinah (Menahem Azariah da Fano, *Kanfei yonah* [Korzec, 1786], pt. 1, sec. 61, 24b). And the daily reading of the biblical account of the binding of Isaac (Genesis 22) is prescribed for the penitent, reciting it with intent and devotion "as though he binds himself upon the altar, asking that the words of his lips be accepted before God as though he were physically slaughtered and prepared and burnt to dust as a sacrificial offering upon the altar" (Fano, *Kanfei yonah*, pt. 2, sec. 109, 57b–58a). The binding of Isaac, the symbolic binding of each and every penitent, makes atonement a possibility (note also *Ḥemdat yamim* [1763] *Yamim noraim* 41a–b). Only a descent to death in one's inner experience suffices to erase one's sins.

However, not in sacrificial offerings, in prayer, in flagellation, or in the devotional reading of the binding of Isaac does the penitent either seek death or believe himself actually to undergo death in the process of penance. Thus, while expressive of a body of teaching and practice, the legend radically transcends it. It appears that the depth of the penance-oriented spirituality that characterized the milieu of

Lurianic Kabbalah—and also of its Sabbatean offshoot—could not find satisfactory expression in the various modes of symbolic death in its practice and thought. Precisely because of its intensity, this penance-oriented spirituality reached out beyond law and accepted religious teaching to the realm of legend, where it could assume the radical form that could not be expressed elsewhere.

The Apostate Who Could Not Sound the Shofar

An apostate could not attain a certain sound on
the shofar until he returned to the Jewish faith.

Once it happened in our days that a shofar blower,[1] a Jew who had converted to another religion, was often in the house where the royal musicians would gather. One day as they were playing their various instruments, he mentioned to them that he knew how to blow one particular horn with a tremendous sound. They requested that he blow it and they brought a shofar, and he began to blow the *tekiah* and *shevarim* with a loud sound. But when he tried, with much effort, to sound the *teruah*,[2] he was unable to do so. He was so perplexed that his heart died within him.

At home he tried again, but again he was unable to do it. He said, "I shall not rest until I know the reason for this," for ever since he had changed his religion he never found the strength to sound the *teruah*. He came to Rabbi Abraham Yakhini[3] to learn the meaning of this thing, and the rabbi answered him, "It is so, and it is explained in the biblical verse, 'Blessed is the people who knows the sound of the *teruah*.'[4] The verse specifies neither *tekiah* nor *shevarim* but only *teruah*, for this is the gift that is given to the people of Israel alone."

. . . And when the convert heard the rabbi's words, his heart melted within him and he lacked the strength even to say, "Woe is me! What have I done? Why have I despised the word of the Lord to turn from Him?" He fled to a distant land and fully repented. Afterward, he tried and was able to sound the *teruah* as he could originally, and he praised God saying, "Blessed is He who chose His people Israel in love";[5] blessed is the people of which this is so; blessed is the people whose God is the Lord."[6]

Ḥemdat yamim, Yamim noraim 43b

1. The shofar, generally a ram's horn, is sounded in the synagogue beginning with the new moon of the month of Elul until the morning prior to Yom Kippur, a period of forty days. It is central to the liturgy and rite of Rosh Hashanah, the observance of the New Year, and is sounded at the conclusion of Yom Kippur.
2. *Tekiah, shevarim,* and *teruah* are the three sounds played on the shofar.

3. An eminent mystic and preacher in Constantinople during the seventeenth century who ultimately headed the followers of Sabbatai Zevi in that city.

4. Psalms 89:16.

5. From the morning liturgy, the blessing preceding the *Shema*.

6. Psalms 144:15. The perplexing situation in the story is understood in the light of the verse from Psalms, which lends this tale a midrashic character.

The situation that the shofar blower could not fathom was itself sufficiently perplexing that the explanation of the rabbi completely shattered the convert's way of life and led him to the radical move of beginning life again as a Jew in another land, a step not uncommon during the times of the Inquisition.

Two expressions of intense shock are translated literally as "his heart melted" and "his heart died within him." While the former suggests a collapse of his will and determination to continue in his adopted faith, the latter adds the nuance of death, which, in turn, interprets his new life as a repentant Jew to be a kind of rebirth.

Could the background of the tale, preserved in a moderate Sabbatean source, point to a polemic against those Sabbateans who had followed Sabbatai Zevi and converted, at least outwardly, to Islam? Such an explanation would provide a contemporary but somewhat problematic context for the tale. The ultimate background of this tale might more likely relate to the period of the Inquisition and the waves of conversions during the last century of Jewish presence in Spain prior to the expulsion in 1492. If so, the purpose of the story is to discourage Jews from the path of conversion even in times of adverse conditions.

The Candle that Blew Out on Yom Kippur

A sign of imminent death, which evokes intense prayer, is followed by a sign of prolonged life.

It once happened that a candle[1] belonging to a rabbi and *Hasid* blew out during the night of Yom Kippur. He was aghast, for he said, "Certainly I am about to die." And in his great distress, he pleaded effusively in prayer with much weeping during the entire Day of Atonement. At night, too, his heart knew no rest, and on the night following Yom Kippur, he clad himself in sackcloth, placed dust upon his head, and repented with great feeling. He cried and pleaded, saying, "Please, Lord, do not take me from the living in the very midst of my days." And on the evening after Yom Kippur he rekindled, before the ark of the Lord in the synagogue, his candle that had previously blown out.

And while it was thought that his candle was of a measure to remain kindled only for the span of a night and a day, miraculously it continued to burn until the night of Hoshanah Rabbah,[2] eleven days later. And it became a sign that his prayer was accepted—that the Lord accepted his supplication and that no evil would befall him.[3]

Ḥemdat yamim, Yamim noraim 65b

1. A candle lit before the beginning of the Day of Atonement signifying the soul of the living person and referred to as a "candle of health." This is not the same as the memorial candle lit just prior to Yom Kippur in memory of the deceased in the family.
2. Eleven days later, regarded as the conclusion of the season of judgment.
3. This tale is included in the text of *Ḥemdat yamim* to confirm the suggestion that if one's candle becomes extinguished during Yom Kippur, one should rekindle it before the ark in the synagogue the following evening.

In *Sefer ḥasidim* (MS Bologne, no. 548), a much earlier work of Jewish ethical literature, it is written that if, during the ten days from Rosh Hashanah to Yom Kippur, one kindles a candle in a place where wind does not enter and if the candle does not blow out, that person will live out the year. Our tale relates to the reverse phenomenon and to the fright resulting from the blowing out of one's candle, which is interpreted as a sign of death.

The story consists of one such sign contradicting another, the second sign being the wondrous lengthening of the time span of the second candle. Repentance on the part of the man whose candle had blown out links the signs of death and life in the story. The reader understands that the extinguishing of the candle was not fortuitous but rather an accurate sign of the man's approaching death. It was his repentance that accounts for the changed verdict. The initial response of the Hasid speaks of his being aghast, literally of "his heart dying within him"; that is, he experiences a psychological death, which is followed by a revival of his spirit after the second sign.

The reader immediately recognizes an echo of the Hanukkah legend found in the Talmud (Shabbat 21b): The candle continued to burn much beyond its normal, expected span of time. The candle motif (Stith Thompson, *Motif-Index of Folk-Literature* (Bloomington, 1955), E761.7.4, life token, light goes out; E765.1.1, life bound up with candle; E761, when candle goes out person dies, and the candle as an example of the life token, which has a mystic relationship with a person's life) recurs in various stories in the literature of this period. *Kav hayashar* (18:6–10) quotes a passage from the introduction to the book *Shibolei haleket*, in which the author, Rabbi Zedekiah ben Abraham Anav, who lived in Italy during the thirteenth century, tells of the wonders that God performed for him when he was deathly ill. In a vision he saw a man standing before him holding a burning candle: The candle began to flicker out but immediately began to burn again. When pressed for an explanation, the man told Rabbi Abraham that the candle symbolizes his soul and that the rekindling of the candle signifies his recovery; and, furthermore, the sick scholar is being judged; but when his deeds are weighed on the scales the judgment is seen to be positive. He is told that God is about to extend his life-span, knowing that he has the capacity to influence many people for good. In three days he will recover from his illness. In fact on the third day, which coincided with the Shavuot festival (the Feast of Weeks), the account continues, he did completely regain his strength. It was then that he began to compose *Shibolei haleket*, his commentary on the liturgy.

Also in *Kav hayashar* (96:4), it is reported that Rabbi Solomon Luria (the *Maharshal*, d. 1574) wrote his book *Yam shel shelomoh*, to the light of a small candle on the verge of being extinguished. But it remained lit for several hours as a sign that God was with him.

From the lore of the world of Lurianic Kabbalah still another legend exemplifies the motif of a light becoming extinguished or flickering as a sign of death. The Ari, it is reported, visited Rabbi Joseph Ashkenazi of Safed on the Sabbath when the latter's candle began to flicker. The guest correctly interpreted this as a sign of the approaching death of his host's son (Meir Benayahu, *Sefer toledot haari* [Jerusalem, 1967] 187–188, no. 29; the letters of Solomon Shlomel of Dreznitz, in Joseph Solomon Delmedigo, *Sefer taalumot ḥokhmah* [Basel, 1629], 44b, quoted also in David Tamar, *Meḥkarim betoledot hayehudim beerets yisrael uveitaliah* [Jerusalem, 1970], 187).

Although this motif is found in tales of many peoples, in Jewish tradition it connects with the biblical verse, "The candle of the Lord is the soul of man" (Proverbs 20:27).

Pride and Humility

The Stench of Pride

A proud person is more odious than
a dead animal.

It happened that a Hasid, walking along the way, met up with Elijah the prophet—may he rest in peace—and, walking together, they came upon an animal carcass that had been thrown out along the path. The carcass gave off such a terrible stench that the Hasid raised his nose to keep from having to smell the animal. Elijah, however, passed close by the carcass without reacting.

Later, they saw a man in the distance coming toward them and walking with a pronounced gait, and though he was still some distance away, Elijah the prophet raised his hand to his nose. When the Hasid asked the prophet why he had not reacted when they passed by the dead animal, Elijah explained that this man, in displaying such pride, gave off a greater stench than did the carcass.

Kav hayashar 7:13

The contrast between humility and arrogance is a recurring theme in Jewish ethical texts beginning with Bahya's *Hovot halevavot: The Sixth Gate.* In this story, the lesson is taught by the prophet Elijah, who, in Jewish lore, had never experienced death and therefore could continually reappear in the world. Often in disguise, he comes to assist people, to test them, or, as in this tale, to teach them. The text surrounding the tale in *Kav hayashar* views humility as a purifying quality, adding that Elijah appeared to the sages of old because they exemplified the virtue of humility.

The Relativity of Wealth

A parable of the relativity of piety.

Two men each have a thousand gold coins. One lives in a village where none of the villagers possess anything approximating that amount of money, and, without doubt, he considers himself superior to his fellow villagers. The other, who resides in a city of many merchants and officials, regards his wealth as amounting to very little, and it is as nothing in his eyes.

Similarly, one who is distant from God and from His holy beings and devout ones considers himself superior to whoever is of a lower level than his. But the pious who are always aware of God's Presence humble themselves to the ground before Him, for in their reflecting upon the level of God and of His holy beings and His devout ones, they are ever humble in their own eyes . . .

Reshit hokhmah, Shaar haahavah 3

This parable from *Reshit hokhmah* exemplifies the characteristic trait of parables from the pietistic literature of the kabbalistic milieu to seek analogies from distant realms of experience. Thus the purely spiritual is illustrated in terms of the most worldly; that is, the quality of holiness in this parable is likened to material wealth.

Reminding Oneself of Death

In bizarre fashion, a man tames his proud will
by reminding himself of death.

It is told of one man who—as reported to the king—would go each night to the cemetery to remove the burial shrouds from corpses in their graves. Before proceeding to bring the accused to trial, the king first sent spies to follow the man and observe his doings. The spies noted that the man would remove a corpse from a grave and then bind himself with a chain to the dead body, shouting and crying while uttering to himself, "My body, my body, know that it is also your end and destiny to be brought to the grave just as happened to this dead person." And he would afflict himself with harsh blows and, in the same spirit, would also recite many ethical passages to subdue his proud will.

All this was reported to the king, who then turned to the man with love and favor. Holding him up as an example for the people of his court, he said, "Do not rely upon your association with the royal court, but rather turn to the Lord." Consequently, they did turn in a complete and perfect repentance.

Mishnat ḥakhamim 19

The textual context of this story in *Mishnat ḥakhamim* refers to talmudic sources that counsel one to remember that one's destiny is death—this as a strategy to counter the evil inclination. However, the story itself appears to have its roots in non-Jewish tradition, since disturbing a body in the grave is clearly incompatible with the norms of Jewish law and practice. For cross-cultural parallels, note Stith Thompson, *Motif-Index of Folk-Literature* (Bloomington, 1955), Q524.2, penance—lying the first night with every corpse brought to a certain church.

Moments of Revelation, of Renewal, and of Failure

The Child's Prophecy

A wonder child utters words of prophecy before
he dies.

Rabbi Pinhas was a very learned man. Although he knew the Ineffable Name, the powerful and awesome Name of God, he had never sinned by using that Name. Many times, however, he was tempted to go with that Name to the land of Edom[1] to uproot their rule from the world. But afterward he was always ashamed of the idea and would say, "I am but a worm and maggot,[2] and how should I transgress the decree of the King of the universe, for He has set an end to darkness in its designated time, as it is written, 'The Lord shall command the host on high in the heights.'[3] And in reflecting in this way he would feel reconciled and cry, saying, "All that the Lord wishes he performs in the heavens and on earth, and so forth."[4]

Now Rabbi Pinhas's wife was Rachel, a very beautiful and a God-fearing woman. She was barren, and after he married her, when she saw that she did not conceive, she turned with money to the wise women asking for medications so that she might conceive. All this, however, was of no avail. Then she prayed to the Lord saying, "Rachel weeps for her children,[5] and I cry for myself," and each day as she awoke in the morning, she washed her face and placed a covering upon her head and cried and did not eat. This persisted for many days.

When her husband, Rabbi Pinhas, came from the academy, she washed his feet and he would go to sleep, and she would eat only once each day, at night. And the holy man, Rabbi Pinhas, had never gazed upon her countenance nor related to her playfully and tenderly.

Rachel prayed and said, "Master of the world, You live and Your Name lives. And I know that in all my days I have never sinned; and even if I have sinned, my husband has not sinned. And even if both of us had sinned, remember on our behalf what You have stated in Your Torah, 'He remembers loving-kindness for the thousandth generation,'[6] and recall, for our benefit, the loving-kindness of Abraham."

She fell upon her face and said, "For the sake of Your Name and Your faithfulness and Your divinity and kingdom, please listen to the prayer of Rachel, Your maidservant." And she wept and shouted, thinking her husband to be asleep. But he heard the sound of her groaning. And Rabbi Pinhas rose and said, "Lord, God of Israel, please hear the prayer of Rachel, Your maidservant," and when Rachel heard this she fell upon her face before her husband, Rabbi Pinhas, and grabbed hold of his feet and said to him, "I swear by the great Name which is known to you that you pray to the Lord to request that He give us a son." Immediately, Rabbi Pinhas stood in trembling and shuddering and he prayed.

The Lord answered him, and his wife, Rachel, conceived and she bore the child for six months. In the seventh month, one Thursday, within an hour after the rising of the morning star, at the beginning of the new moon marked by the sign of just and righteous scales,[7] on the first day of the month of Tishri, four hundred twenty years after the destruction of the Second Temple, she gave birth. She named the child Nahman,[8] and just as soon as he was born he bowed before his mother and said, "Above this vault of the heavens that you see there are nine hundred fifty-five domes, and above them are four beasts, and above them the high and exulted Throne, and above the Throne a consuming fire, and His precious Throne and all His servants are fire."[9]

When Rabbi Pinhas, his father, heard these words, he rebuked and silenced him, and the child became mute and did not speak for twelve years. His mother would cry and say, "I had a son, but would that I never had a son." And the lad, Nahman, was very handsome.

One day as Rabbi Pinhas came from the academy, his wife Rachel rose and washed his feet as was her custom. And afterward she brought her son, the lad Nahman, and placed him in his father's bosom; and she bowed down to the ground holding her husband's feet and cried and kissed the soles of his feet saying, "I beg you, either allow him to speak or let him die." That very moment, Rabbi Pinhas beheld the lad's face and saw that he was exceedingly handsome, and he bowed down and kissed him three times. When Rachel saw this she became calm and Rabbi Pinhas said to her, "Get up, why do you bow down?" And she had never been disobedient to him and had never transgressed his word, and also he, in turn, had never angered her nor treated her playfully. And as she stood up on her feet, Rabbi Pinhas said to her, "What is your wish concerning this lad?" She responded, "My wish is that which will be pleasing to our Maker." Rabbi Pinhas said to her, "I know that your wish is that I permit him to speak." "Yes, my master," she said, falling at his feet and pleading with him to do so. Rabbi Pinhas said to her, "What a pity that the lad who is so wise and so intelligent has so few days to live, and his mother requests that I permit him to speak while I know that he will say things that will appall people." Rachel responded, "My master, allow him to speak secretly, in a way that others will not comprehend."

Rabbi Pinhas put his mouth to the lad's mouth and commanded him not to speak clearly and openly but rather in speech that is sealed from understanding so that no person, even a wise man, might understand him until the time comes for his word to be fulfilled. Afterward he told the lad, "You are now permitted to speak." The lad then opened his mouth and, through him, the Lord spoke prophecies in alphabetical order. And when he completed his utterance his father said to him, "Be strong and have courage."[10]

Nahman answered saying, "Father and mother, you shall live long, but you will bury me, your last child." His father and mother cried from that day until the day of his death, for he soon died, leaving this life for the life of the world to come. This was the story of Nahman Hatufa of the village, Baram,[11] and with him, in a cave, are forty righteous and saintly ones . . .[12]

Printed at end of *Naggid umetsaveh*

1. Rome and Byzantium.
2. Mishnah Avot 3:1. Realizing his humble position vis-à-vis God, he must be careful to refrain from utilizing his mystic knowledge and power even for the purpose of saving his people.
3. Isaiah 24:21.
4. Psalms 135:6.
5. Jeremiah 31:15, referring to the matriarch Rachel, weeping for her descendants as they are carried away into exile.
6. Exodus 34:7.
7. The sign of the month of Tishri, the seventh month of the year according to the biblical order of counting the months. The sign relates to the season of divine judgment.
8. From *n-ḥ-m* (comfort, consolation).
9. In the style of Ezekiel 1.
10. Joshua 1:6.
11. Situated seven miles northwest of Safed. The village, destroyed in the eighteenth century, is the site of a third-century synagogue, the remains of which have been partially restored.
12. Now, in the world to come.

This story is followed in the text by five extremely cryptic prophecies in Aramaic. According to the account, the prophecies should be dated 502 C.E., calculated on the basis of the number of years since the destruction of the Second Temple, as mentioned in the story. Some scholars have suggested that the writing of these prophecies can be dated as early as the thirteenth or fourteenth centuries and that they relate to events in the Near East in that earlier period (Gershom Scholem, "Rabi avraham ben eliezer halevi," *Kiriat Sefer* 2 [1925–1926]: 117; Eli Strauss, *Toledot hayehudim bemitsrayim vesuria* 1 [Jerusalem, 1960], 129). The story was already known close to the time of the expulsion from Spain, and Abraham ben Eliezer ha-Levi wrote a commentary on the prophecies early in the sixteenth century (Scholem, "Rabi avraham," pp. 115–117). This work, which exists only in manuscript, interprets the prophecies as referring to the imminent coming of the Messiah amid catastrophic events (Scholem, "Rabi avraham ben eliezer helevi"). Joseph Dan ("Lekutot lemaasei nevuat hayeled," *Shalem* 1 [1974]: 229–234) relates this story to the same background of messianic tensions and expectations that produced the story of Joseph della Reina—also found in the writings of Abraham ben Eliezer ha-Levi. Both accept the possibility and legitimacy of utilizing magic to hasten redemption. These and other stories of that nature appear to have flourished, especially in kabbalistic circles, in Jerusalem in the early sixteenth century and later in Safed (Dan, "Lekutot lemaasei nevuat heyeled," pp. 230–231).

The narrative that introduces the prophecies displays an affinity with the world of the zoharic story, recalling the motif of the *yenuka*, the wonder child, found in the Zohar, with its suggestion of innocence and knowledge. The Zohar states not only that children are, at times, capable of prophecy but also that they prophesy even more than the bibilical prophets (Zohar 2:170a). Even the cave mentioned at the end of the narrative bears an association with the cave in which Rabbi Simeon bar Yohai and his son Eleazer hid from the Romans (according to a rabbinic tradition elaborated upon in the basic ongoing story in the Zohar).

The narrative recalls the biblical accounts of prolonged childlessness and the birth of a child only after a long period of time and intense longing for a child. The name Rachel, in fact, points to the biblical matriarch, who was among those who waited long and impatiently for a child. The motif echoes also in Christian legend in which wonder children are born to mothers who, it was believed, could not bear children (C. Grant Loomis, *White Magic* [Cambridge, Mass., 1948], 20). Compare also Stith Thompson, *Motif-Index of*

Folk-Literature (Bloomington, 1955), Q. 192: "Child Given as Reward for Prayer" and T. 526: "Conception Because of Prayer." Unlike the pattern in the biblical narratives, however, the eventual birth of a son to Rachel and Pinhas is followed by the tragedy of the child's early death. The danger involved in messianic calculations, at times closely associated with mystical knowledge, is not lessened when it is associated with the innocence of a child prophet. On the contrary, as we see, it exacts a double cost: muteness and death for the child and ongoing sorrow for his parents.

Dan also points to a parallel that likely had indirect influence upon the origins of the story in the account of Merlin from the Arthurian cycle of legends. That account, found as early as the twelfth century in a Latin source, tells of Merlin's miraculous birth and of his powers of prophecy concerning historical events, prophecies delivered in cryptic language and imagery that was unintelligible to his listeners (Dan, *"Lekutot lemaasei nevuat hayeled,"* pp. 233–234).

In the address delivered on the occasion of receiving an honorary doctorate from the Hebrew University, S. Y. Agnon mentioned that in his youth in Galicia he had written an epic based upon "The Child's Prophecy," a work, however, that was not preserved (*Haaretz*, May 2, 1958). Eventually "The Child's Prophecy," along with the account of the biblical Rachel, would echo in the last portion of his novel, *A Guest for the Night* (1968; Original Hebrew, *Oreah natah lalun*, 1938–1939), when a son is born to Rachel and Yeruham Hofshi following a span of several months in which not one child was born to the Jewish inhabitants of the Galician town of Scibucz. In that novel, the birth of Rachel's son interrupts a prolonged period of collective barrenness and signifies a kind of rebirth of the persona after whom the infant is named. See Arnold J. Band, *Nostalgia and Nightmare* (Berkeley and Los Angeles, 1968), 326–327; and Aryeh Wineman, *Aggadah veomanut* (Jerusalem, 1982), 20–21.

The Revelation of the Shekhinah by the Western Wall

The Shekhinah reveals Herself as one who suffers and consoles.

Long after Jeremiah, with the exile of the Shekhinah,[1] went about composing lamentations concerning the Temple fortress and the Holy One, blessed be He, and His Shekhinah, there lived one of the great ones of the Holy Land. This was our teacher and rabbi, Abraham ha-Levi,[2] a Hasid, a holy man, and a recluse for the sake of Torah during all his days. . . . And our Rabbi, the Ari—may his memory be for a blessing—would speak at length of the high spiritual level of the former, and he grasped through his inspired knowledge that ha-Levi was a spark of the soul of Jeremiah the prophet, may he rest in peace.

One day, when that righteous man had taken ill and was approaching the very gates of death, the Rabbi—may his memory be for a blessing—came to visit him in his home and told him: "Behold the time of your death is near; nevertheless I will instruct you for the purpose of helping you, and if you follow my instruction, another twenty-two years will be added to your life. Agree, now, to go to pray at the Western Wall and to pour out your supplication there, and you will be privileged to see the countenance of the Shekhinah. Then you will immediately be healed of your illness." He immediately vowed to go, according to the Rabbi's instruction, and at once he was cured of his disease.

Then he sold the furnishings from his house for the expenses of his journey, for he was exceptionally poor. He went to Jerusalem and came to the Western Wall and rent his garments as is proper for one who sees the Temple site in ruin. And immediately the Shekhinah revealed Herself to him. He saw Her—if it is possible to say so—just as Jeremiah the prophet had seen Her, departing from the Holy of Holies with Her head disheveled. . . . And since the Hasid Rabbi Abraham—may he rest in peace—saw Her in such great distress, he cried aloud with raised voice[3] and with a great and bitter shout. Gravely distressed, he ran toward a house there and struck his head against the walls of the house and fainted out of his deep sorrow. He fell to the ground, and then he saw that the Shekhinah took his head between Her knees and wiped the tears from his eyes. And She said to him,

"Abraham, my son, be consoled, for there is hope for your future, and the children will return to their border."[4]

Afterward, when his spirit revived, he returned to Safed. He came before the Rabbi (the Ari), who asked him, "Have you seen such and such?" And he answered him, "Yes." And he said to Rabbi Abraham, "All this you have seen through the merit of the repentance that you helped to awaken, and as a consequence God will add twenty-two years to your life[5] for the sake of the Shekhinah, the mystery of the Oral Torah that is composed of twenty-two letters,[5] and for the sake of the soul of Jeremiah, the prophet—may he rest in peace—which is with you. Be strong and mighty in your awe of the Lord to continue to awaken repentance among the townspeople, for in the merit of even one such gathering for repentance, the exile is subdued. And his soul will help you in these holy tasks . . ."

Ḥemdat yamim, Rosh ḥodesh 4a

1. The Divine Presence. In rabbinic sources the term serves as an expression of the immanence of God (Efraim E. Urbach, *Ḥazal: Pirke emunot vedeot* [Jerusalem, 1969], 50–52), whereas in the kabbalistic world view the Shekhinah is the tenth of the *sefirot*, the forms or aspects assumed by the divine light and being.

2. Abraham ben Eliezer ha-Levi Berukhim (1515–1593) was born in Morocco and settled in Safed during the 1560s. (He is not to be confused with the earlier Abraham ben Eliezer ha-Levi, a native of Spain who died in Jerusalem about 1530.) He became a follower of Rabbi Moses Cordovero, but like several others in that circle he associated himself, following Cordovero's death, with the followers of the Ari. His activity in Safed in awakening his townspeople both to the observance of the Sabbath and to participation in the midnight vigil (*tikkun ḥatsot*) is noted in several of the popular pietistic texts (*Kav hayashar* 93; *Shivḥei haari* included in Meir Benayahu, *Sefer toledot haari* [Jerusalem, 1967], 228–230; *Ḥemdat yamim* [1763] *Rosh ḥodesh* 4a). In *Sefer haḥezionot* (ed. Aharon Z. Eshkoli, [Jerusalem, 1954], 130), the mystical autobiography written by Rabbi Hayyim Vital, the author described him as one who could move people to repentance even against their will. He also mentions that the name of Elijah the prophet, who is to appear prior to the Messiah's coming, has been changed to Abraham and it is through his efforts that the redemption will come.

3. The Hebrew words suggest *kol beramah nishma* ("A voice is heard in Ramah," Jeremiah 31:14).

4. Jeremiah 31:16.

5. Stith Thompson, *Motif-Index of Folk Literature* (Bloomington, 1955), D. 1855: "Time of Death Postponed."

6. The twenty-two years added to Berukhim's life relate to the kabbalistic association of the Shekhinah with the Oral Torah, often as a personification of the Mishnah, composed of the twenty-two letters of the Hebrew alphabet (Note R. J. Zwi Werblowsky, *Joseph Karo: Lawyer and Mystic* [Oxford, 1962], 265–268). The

version of the legend in *Emek hamelekh* explains the twenty-two years as relating to "the Shekhinah who is the Oral Torah which is constructed of twenty-two letters . . ." (*Emek hamelekh* [1648] 109b). One finds mention of twenty-two years added to one's life in the Zohar (3:205ab).

The various versions of this legend (the epistles of Solomon Shlomel of Dreznitz, printed in Abraham Yaari, *Iggarot erets yisrael* [Ramat Gan, 1971], 205–206; Benayahu, *Sefer toledot haari*, pp. 228–230; *Emek hamelekh* [1648] 109b; *Kav hayashar* 93; *Or hayashar, Amud haavodah* 11 [1709] 7b; *Ḥemdat yamim* [1763] *Rosh ḥodesh* 4a) identify Rabbi Abraham ha-Levi as a metempsychosis of Jeremiah or, as in the text in *Ḥemdat yamim*, as having a spark of the prophet's soul. In addition, the encounter between the rabbi and the Shekhinah in the legend appears as a refraction of the brief narrative in Jeremiah 31:14–16.

Several works from earlier periods include the highly symbolic figure of a woman weeping and mourning at the scene of the destruction of Jerusalem. In the Apocalypse of Ezra (known also as 4 Ezra or 2 Esdras; Robert H. Charles, *The Apocrypha and the Pseudepigrapha of the Old Testament*, vol. 2 [Oxford, 1913] 603ff.), Pesikta Rabbati 26:7, and a lament, *Az bimlot sefek yafah ketirtsah* by Eleazar Kallir (*Seder megilat ekha utfilat lel tishah beav ukinot keminhag ashkenazim upolin* [Mantua, 1720], 22; Heinrich Brody, ed., *Anthologica hebraica*, [Leipzig, 1922], 44; listed in Israel Davidson, *Thesaurus of Medieval Hebrew Poetry*, vol. 1 [New York, 1924–1933], no. 2108), very dissimilar sources, the woman is seen weeping bitterly with all the marks of bereavement. She is identified as Mother Zion, and except for the last-mentioned source, the text consists of a dual vision representing Jerusalem both destroyed and rebuilt. In the light of all the above sources, the legend of Rabbi Abraham ha-Levi Berukhim appears to be one expression of a legend-tradition that has spanned a millennium and a half, one that has recast the biblical dialogue between God and Rachel into a dialogue involving the figure of a woman in mourning who symbolizes Jerusalem and Israel. By the time of the Berukhim legend she transcends that role and is identified as the Shekhinah.

A sign in that development can be heard in a passage from Tana Devei Eliyahu, which explicates the verses from Jeremiah 31, "Read this not as *raḥel* [Rachel] weeping for her children but, rather as *ruaḥ-el* [the spirit of God] weeping for her children" (Tana Devei Eliyahu, [Jerusalem, 1959] Seder Eliyahu Rabba, vol. 2, chapter 30,

p. 442). It is the divine who mourns the exile and the destruction of Jerusalem, an extension of a tendency in rabbinic thought that emphasizes God's empathy with the plight of Israel and His unceasing grief over the destruction of the Temple (Berakhot 3a; Lamentations *Rabba*, proems 24 and 25; Tana Devei Eliyahu, Seder Eliyahu Rabbah, vol. 2, chapter 30; Peter Kuhn, *Gottes Trauer und Klage in der rabbinischen Überlieferung* [Leiden, 1978]). In the Zohar's interpretation of that same passage from Jeremiah, it is explicitly the Shekhinah who weeps (Zohar 1:203a; note also Zohar 3:20b)—the older legend-tradition has acquired a new dimension in the world view of Kabbalah. As the Shekhinah is a feminine *sefirah*, it is the logical candidate for the role of the weeping woman at the scene of the destruction of Jerusalem. In the Zoharic exegesis (of the Bible), many female figures from the pentateuchal narratives serve to symbolize the Shekhinah, regarded as a divine prototype of the people of Israel (Zohar 3:20b). That connection with Israel is emblematic of the continuity with older versions of the same basic legend-tradition.

The dual epiphany, the Shekhinah in mourning and the Shekhinah offering consolation, likewise recalls the pattern of some of the prekabbalistic statements of that tradition. Notwithstanding the similarities, however, certain significant role reversals are evident in the Berukhim legend. Unlike the passage in Jeremiah 31 and the examples from the Apocrypha, the Midrash, and *piyyut*, the female figure is not actually weeping. It is, rather, the man, Rabbi Abraham ha-Levi Berukhim, who weeps while the Shekhinah consoles him. The legend thus voices not divine empathy for the plight of Israel's exiles but rather the empathy of the Jew for the divine and for the exile experienced by the divine. Divine empathy has given way to the theme of the exile of the Shekhinah, and in depicting the divine dimension and suffering the legend has become infinitely more appalling, even as, in daring legendary expression, it has moved to the brink of experiencing the divine in human form.

A further difference: Unlike all the older examples, the vision and encounter in the Berukhim legend do not occur at the time of the destruction of Jerusalem. Rather, they occur very close to the time of the legend's actual appearance since the tale relates to two historical personalities who could both have been present together in Safed only from 1570 to 1572, during the very last years of the Ari's life. The legend speaks, therefore, not of the remote past but of its own time.

Rabbi Abraham ben Eliezer ha-Levi, the historical figure, is closely associated with the practice of the midnight vigil in Safed. This ritual is a lament for the destruction of the Temple and the exile of the Shekhinah, even though its ultimate meaning transcends the element of grief by an act of repair aimed at annulling the fact of exile. The rhythm of the legend voices the basic formula underlying that rite: The quest to experience most intensely the sorrow of exile and the exile of the Shekhinah also constitutes the way to annul that sorrow and that exile. The way to *tikkun,* the repair of sin and exile, lies in immersing oneself in grief. As the weeping figure in the legend, Berukhim suggests the role of the Jew in lamenting the exile of the Shekhinah, and the legend serves as a paradigm of such lament and its significance.

Placed in the sixteenth century rather than at the time of the destruction of Jerusalem, the legend stresses redemption rather than past destruction. This note is voiced forcefully though subtly in the Ari's identification of Rabbi Abraham ha-Levi Berukhim as a metempsychosis of the prophet Jeremiah—with all its particular ramifications for the legend. That identification may well have been the genesis of the Berukhim legend, for we are told that the Ari also identified others of his contemporaries as metempsychoses of significant figures from biblical and talmudic times (Benayahu, *Sefer toledot haari,* pp. 155, 164, 189, 258).

The identification of Berukhim with Jeremiah implies a comparison of the prophet's generation with that of the Hasid from Safed: Jeremiah had failed to bring his contemporaries to the kind of repentance that would have averted the destruction and the consequent exile, whereas Abraham ha-Levi Berukhim succeeded in large measure in awakening his own generation to repentance. That awakening is represented by their participation in the midnight vigil—which echoes the biblical Book of Lamentations traditionally ascribed to Jeremiah—and in the study session following the vigil. The very act of a physical awakening from slumber parallels an inner spiritual awakening. Berukhim's endeavor bore significantly greater fruit and, hence, also offered the promise of awakening divine compassion. That comparison is, indeed, made explicit in *Ḥemdat yamim* [1763] *Rosh ḥodesh* 4a, ". . . Whereas when Jeremiah used to rebuke Israel they neither listened nor inclined the ear, now [Rabbi Abraham's] fear and awe fell upon all Jews, all of whom accepted his discipline . . ."

The age of Jeremiah is associated with the exile of the

Shekhinah. The movement of repentance with its ascetic rites in the time of Berukhim suggests, by contrast, the sense of imminent redemption and the restoration of the Shekhinah to Her former glory. The older legend-tradition that lies behind this story has been so radically refashioned that the very scene of the destruction of Jerusalem and of the exile of the Divine Presence becomes the scene of a promise of imminent redemption in the wake of the expressions of repentance and spiritual awakening in the community of Safed.

The Journey that Did Not Take Place

Lack of unanimity and wholeness among the master's students means the loss of an opportune moment for divine redemption.

Late one Friday afternoon, just prior to the arrival of the Sabbath bride,[1] the Rabbi (the Ari)—may he rest in peace—went with his students beyond the edge of the town of Safed—may it be built and established quickly in our days—dressed in four white garments[2] in order to welcome the Sabbath.

He had begun to chant "A Psalm of David, Ascribe to the Lord, you sons of the mighty,"[3] along with a special melody for the welcoming of the Sabbath.[4] They hummed, "A Song for the Sabbath Day,"[5] a lovely melody. As they were chanting the Rabbi remarked to his pupils, "Friends,[6] is it your will that we go to Jerusalem prior to the Sabbath and that we begin the Sabbath in Jerusalem?"—Jerusalem being more than twenty-five parasangs[7] from Safed. Some of the students responded, "We are ready to obey," while others requested, "Let us go first to inform our wives, and afterward we will make the journey."

Then he trembled profoundly, clapping his hands together and saying, "Woe to us in that we do not merit redemption. For since you were not ready[8] in this matter, the exile has returned to its full force because of our many iniquities—had you all responded of one accord that you were willing to go joyously, then immediately all Israel would have been redeemed. For redemption was near because that moment was one in which divine compassion was awakened above."

Ḥemdat yamim, Shabbat 40a

---

1. The Sabbath is likened to a bride (Genesis Rabba 11:8) and hence the welcoming or receiving of the Sabbath is a symbolic wedding between the people of Israel and the seventh day as its bride. See also Israel Al-Nakawa, *Menorat hamaor*, vol. 2 (ed. Hyman G. Enelow [New York, 1929–1934], 191). The Talmud reports that Yannai, a third-century sage, used to clad himself in white garments on the eve of the Sabbath and say, "Come, O Bride, come, O Bride" (Shabbat 119a). The image of the Sabbath as a bride is central to the refrain of *Lekha dodi*, the poem to mark the welcoming of the Sabbath composed in Safed in the sixteenth century.

2. The wearing of unspecified special garments for the Sabbath is found already

in a talmudic source, Shabbat 25b. The Ari clad himself in four white garments corresponding to the four letters of the Ineffable Name (David Tamar, *Bikoret umasa, ishim usefarim* [Jerusalem, 1973], 40). A document included in Solomon Schechter's *Studies in Judaism: Second Series* ([Philadelphia, 1908], 299–300) mentions in the directions for the spiritual life received from Rabbi Moses of Lirea three explanations of the wearing of white garments on the Sabbath: In doing so one resembles an angel of God; souls clad themselves in white, in garments of light; and both the Lord and the Divine Presence remove black garments, which represent the quality of judgment, and clad themselves in white garments, which represent the opposite quality of compassion.

3. Psalms 29:1. This is the last of a group of six psalms added to the welcoming of the Sabbath to represent the six days of the week prior to the Sabbath. While the addition of these psalms to the liturgy is generally ascribed to the Safed Kabbalists of the sixteenth century, Abraham J. Heschel (*The Sabbath* [New York, 1951], 113 n. 6) raises the possibility that it might date back to an earlier period.

4. Presumably, *Lekha dodi*, "Come, my beloved, to greet the bride; let us welcome the Sabbath," written in Safed by Solomon Alkabez.

5. Psalm 92.

6. Members of a *ḥavurah,* or group of associates, devoted to study and the pursuit of spirituality.

7. Approximately four miles each, making for a total distance of one hundred miles between Safed and Jerusalem.

8. The term *miun* (unwillingness, refusal) is associated in talmudic law with a refusal of a female minor to enter into an arranged betrothal, an overtone that subtly strengthens the allusion to the marriage theme in the legend.

In kabbalistic literature, the Sabbath is in one sense perceived as a celebration and experience of reality redeemed. The wedding imagery itself is suggestive of redemption, which is understood ultimately as an act of divine union. The legend is built upon the tension between the welcoming of the Sabbath, suggesting redemption, and the bitterness of the disappointment that follows. Instead of *ḥazarah biteshuvah* (return and repentance) on the part of Israel, it is the exile that has returned (*ḥ-z-r*) in full force. Of the joy of the Sabbath voiced in song in the opening, nothing remains at the end. That ecstatic joy gives way to fright and shock. The reader can presume that had the Ari's followers been carried away by the joy of ushering in the Sabbath, the practical considerations such as they posed would not have been raised. These only indicate, according to the logic of the legend, that his followers were not completely immersed in the Sabbath experience.

In some earlier forms of this legend, appearing in the various collections (Meir Benayahu, *Sefer toledot haari* [Jerusalem, 1967], 168–169, and the parallels cited there), those who hesitated did so because of the distance separating Jerusalem from Safed, since they had but a moment's notice before setting out on the lengthy journey. In *Ḥemdat yamim* and also in *Emek hamelekh* (1648), Introduction, 11d–12a, they hesitated to proceed without first informing their wives. Hence our text takes a more radical position: None of the followers opposed the journey to Jerusalem because of factors of distance and time; the opposition grew out of their wish to inform their wives—seemingly a reasonable consideration—before undertaking the wondrous journey. The legend presumes that the presence of a true will to undertake the trip would cancel rational and natural considerations and obstacles. Thus we are told that were it their true will to go to Jerusalem at that moment, the redemption would have come immediately, obviating at the same time any earthly problems or concerns.

This legend operates on two different levels: the human and the divine. In the first part the joy and the responses to the Ari's suggestion occur in the human realm. The legend then discloses how those same events are experienced above: The divided response of the students leads to an utter rejection because the moment had not been an ordinary moment but one propitious for redemption. Consequently the response—or lack of response—assumes a significance of radical and frightful dimensions. What is perceived below as an ordinary moment and response is viewed above as a pivotal and potentially fatal moment. The last word in the Hebrew text of the legend is, appropriately, *lemaalah* (above). It is the Ari who reveals to his students the significance of their response as grasped from a perspective that transcends the world of human experience.

The Seven Shepherds
Called to the Torah Reading

An awesome scene evokes in a student a response
of laughter, which thwarts an opportune moment
of divine redemption.

It happened one holy Sabbath that the Rabbi (the Ari) said to his friends, "If you agree not to speak at all during the course of the morning prayer in the synagogue until after leaving the synagogue and if not one of you laughs at anything you see, then I will pray with you today and will lead the prayers, and I will call the seven shepherds[1] to the reading of the Torah."[2]

The pupils answered, "We will do as our master commands." He said to them, "Behold I see that one of you will certainly be punished for laughing." Nevertheless they implored him at great length until he agreed to go ahead.

They came to the synagogue where the Rabbi led the morning prayer, and at the time of the taking out of the Torah scroll from the ark, the friends saw angels in the synagogue, ascending and descending[3] with vivaciousness and gladness and joy. The Ari called upon Aaron the priest,[4] who then came and read the opening portion himself with a lovely melody, wondrously holy, and recited the blessings before and after. Similarly, for the Levite portion,[5] the Ari called upon Moses, who then read the passage with an exceedingly strong voice. Following him he called upon Abraham, Isaac, and Jacob, and he called also upon Joseph the righteous[6] to be the sixth.

And for the seventh, he called upon David, the son of Jesse, who then appeared, jumping and dancing with all his strength before the ark of the covenant of the Lord,[7] clad in a cloth ephod[8] and wearing a cloth garment upon his loins as he had when he brought the ark of the Lord up to Jerusalem.

But upon seeing him jumping and dancing, one student broke out in laughter and was punished[9] and died that same year. It had been the intent of the Rabbi to gather together the seven shepherds in one group and to pray with them the additional prayer[10] in order to awaken the heavenly compassion and to restore the crown to its former position.[11]

But what will the sages do whose generation is not equal to that of the Ari? It is well to reflect upon the deeds of the great ones with awe and fear and trembling, for we have lost much that is good.

Ḥemdat yamim, Shabbat 81a

1. Abraham, Isaac, Jacob, Joseph, Moses, Aaron, and David. Messianic associations of the seven shepherds motif are found in Sukkah 52a and in the Targums on Deuteronomy 33:5. According to a talmudic tradition (Bava Metsia 85a), the three patriarchs are not permitted to pray together, for were they to do so, God could not prevent the Messiah's coming before his time in the face of the force of their collective prayer.

2. Seven Jews are called to the reading of the Torah each Saturday morning, in addition to an eighth who then reads the prophetic portion.

3. Genesis 28:12.

4. The priest (*kohen*) is the first to be called to the Torah. Aaron, Moses's brother, was the first priest in Israel.

5. The second to be called to the Torah reading must be from the tribe of Levi, the tribe of Moses.

6. In midrashic sources in particular, Joseph is referred to as "Joseph, the righteous" in view of his withstanding illicit temptation while working as a servant in Egypt.

7. Reference to 2 Samuel 6:16.

8. Official priestly garment worn by the High Priest (Exodus 28:31).

9. Or "afflicted with incurable illness."

10. Musaf, following the Torah reading on the Sabbath and on special occasions.

11. Fulfilling the task of *tikkun*, of mending the shattered unity of the divine worlds and hence bringing, in its wake, a messianic restoration of Israel's former glory in the world.

This legend is found in much briefer form in *Emek hamelekh* (1648, third Introduction, 7:13a) and is another of the subgenre of the Ari legends that convey the failure to respond properly to a potentially redemptive moment. The text in *Ḥemdat yamim* represents a considerable expansion of the earlier versions of this same tradition.

The tragic foreknowledge of the inability to fulfill the Ari's terms lends a distinct dramatic quality to the legend. Understood, as in the previous legend, is the requirement of unanimity on the part of all the students. Hence even one member of the circle who is incapable of responding properly dooms the entire endeavor.

Why did the Ari put his students to the test knowing in advance what the results would be? The question is left unanswered.

In the text the verb *reeh* (see) occurs with two distinct meanings: The students are going to see wondrous events and phenomena; and the Ari foresees that one of the group will break the code of conduct and be struck down. The two are linked together: The sight of such wonders without the inner capacity to relate to them properly culminates in severe affliction.

When the Ari offers his suggestion, the text refers to the students as *haverim* (friends, associates), on the same level as the Ari, who speaks to them, as it were, as his equals, those who fully share his level of concern and spiritual commitment. He will pray, he tells them, "with you," the phrase similarly suggesting togetherness and proximity if not full equality. The "pupils" respond, accepting the mandate obediently. The use of the word *naase* (we will do) recalls Exodus 24:7, in which the Israelites indicate to Moses their commitment to obey the teaching he will relay to them. After the master's warning that one of the group would fail the test and be severely punished, they nevertheless pleaded with him to go through with the original suggestion, and in that state of self-certainty they are referred to as *talmidim* (pupils)—not *haverim*. The former word connotes, by comparison, a distance between the master and his circle of students. When he actually prays with the students, it is written only that "he prayed" without the words "with them." In beholding the angels and wonders, the students are again referred to as *haverim,* but at the moment of failure, it is a *talmid* who breaks out laughing. The words thus suggest an alternation between proximity and distance in the ambivalent relationship between the Rabbi and his circle of students.

The Ari's intent is disclosed only at the end of the legend—he had never defined it to the students. Having perceived things on one level, while the Rabbi grasped them on a very different level, it follows that the students never comprehended the gravity of the experiment, yet another mark of the distance separating them.

The ambivalence and overall context of the legend suggest that the distance of the pupil who laughs during the sacred experience represents the great distance of the group as a whole from the Ari and his level of spirituality. They lack the necessary inner readiness even as they urge him to allow them to accept his mandate. Proceeding one step further, one also might suggest that the failure of the group, in turn, is emblematic of the distance of the entire generation from its vocation of *tikkun.*

Except for joining in the prayer, the students were to remain silent in the synagogue, silence being a fence around laughter and profane light-headedness. Only such silence allows for a holy response to a holy event. The flaw, the laughter of the transgressing pupil, is the antithesis of silence.

It is fitting in terms of narrative logic that the temptation should arise with David, the last of the seven shepherds. The legend implies that David's jumping and leaping occurred in a state of holiness and, hence, should not have occasioned laughter. The challenge was to experience the joyous motions of King David as nothing less than sacred joy—with all the gravity that inheres in a sacred act. Had the entire circle of students grasped this joy correctly, redemption could have occurred. As David relived the historic moment when the ark was returned to Jerusalem to end its exile, so the present moment could have been one of return marking the end of exile in its broader sense. The student's failing was his inability to submerge the entire self in the sacred nature of the joy of that hour. Instead, he related to it as secular joy, divorced from the sacred.

Given the milieu that spawned this legend, one overhears something of a cultural comment: Just as David's jumping and dancing occurred in a state of holiness (and hence constitutes no reason to elicit a light-headed response), similarly poetry and song should not occasion frivolity or laughter but should inspire a mood of awe and holiness (note *Hemdat yamim* [1763] *Shabbat* 71a and 94b). The identical expression, *mefazezim umkarkarim* (jumping and dancing), occurs in the same volume (103a) in describing the former practice of the pious followers of the great rabbis of Germany and France during the last hour of the Sabbath. The conclusion, then, is that art and beauty are not to serve as an escape from the gravity of life's ultimate task nor as an occasion for levity or laughter. Rather, as seen through the perspective of the text's pietistic view of culture, beauty is to be experienced in a state of awe before omnipresent God.

The motif of calling the seven shepherds to the Torah reading came to be associated in legend also with the fourteenth-century Rabbi Isaac Aboab, author of *Menorat hamaor*. In a written source from a later period (*Maasiyot mitsadikei yesodei olam* [Pedgorna, 1903], nos. 1,2) it is told that Aboab—while on a journey to examine a Torah scroll written by Ezra himself in order to clarify the exact letters in certain verses of the Torah—had to spend the Sabbath at a small village. During the morning prayer there, one of the villagers called the seven shepherds, who consequently appeared and read from the Torah those very verses concerning which Rabbi Aboab was uncertain.

In 1774, Rabbi Simhah ben Joshua Zalozhtsy wrote (*Sippurei erets hagalil,* also called *Ahavat tsion,* included in Judah D. Eisenstein, *Otsar masaot* [New York, 1926], 237ff.) that the reading desk in the synagogue from which the Ari called the seven shepherds to the Torah reading survived the earthquake that later destroyed most of Safed's synagogues.

Some Parables of the Wise

Blindness and Light

I

*Having known the divine light, the soul is no
longer content with darkness.*

When a person becomes blind—one who had previously been able to
experience the sweetness of light—he never gives up waiting for the
screen of blindness to be removed from his eyes by means of one
medical drug or another, so that once again he may be able to perceive
the bright light.

Similarly, the soul is hewed from the light of divine life in the
higher worlds; and when God placed it in this unseemly body, as in a
prison,[1] it could then no longer behold the higher lights. And so the
understanding person will turn to the holiness of the Torah and the
mitzvot as remedies. . . . And through them his soul will be hallowed
and will cleave to the bright light, the light of the Torah, which is
referred to as "light," as it is written, "And the Torah is light."[2] And
he will turn to God in order to remove the screen separating him from
his God . . .

Reshit ḥokhmah, Shaar haahavah 11

1. The view that the soul is a prisoner of the body, akin to that found in Plato,
entered Jewish thought largely through Bahya ibn Paguda's eleventh-century work,
Ḥovot halevavot, which left its imprint upon much of later ethical literature.
2. Proverbs 6:23.

II

*Each day of the week must contain something of
the quality of the Sabbath; otherwise, a person is
incapable of truly experiencing the Sabbath in its
own time.*

Each day a person must hallow himself with the holiness that belongs to the Sabbath so that when the Sabbath does come, he will be capable of receiving its holiness. It is like the person who is in a dark place: If he should go out to the light and see the bright sunlight, his eyes would close and he would be unable to enjoy its sweet light. . . . The light of dawn begins to shine only gradually and the same is true of the light of Sabbath holiness.[1]

Reshit ḥokhmah, Shaar hakedushah 7

1. This passage immediately brings to mind the analogy of the cave in Plato's *Republic* 6, which similarly speaks of one accustomed to darkness who suddenly sees light.

A Tale of Two Slaves

A wise man seeks a truthful master to guide him with good judgment, and he prospers. A fool who seeks only easily obtained food brings ruin to his house.

It once happened that two men went to the marketplace, each one seeking to purchase a slave. When they came to the trading block where servants were sold they found there only one man, poor in appearance and clad in ragged clothes. (Actually he was a person marked by misfortune but also by wisdom.) One of these two men drew near to him and asked that poor man up for sale whom he would want to purchase him. "Tell me," he asked, "what is your work and what do you do? For with that consideration I have come to acquire one who will be my servant for years to come." The slave responded, "I know how to guide you and all the members of your household and all who are attached to you and to chastise you justly. I will be your servant only on the prior condition that even you, as master, will be subject to my direction and judgment and will serve me and listen to my words of criticism."

Now the servant's words were as a laughing matter in the man's eyes and he mocked him thinking, "How presumptuous of him to speak this way!" He spit in the face of that servant who was up for sale and walked away, seeing in him either an utter fool or one who is out of his mind. "Does a person being sold as a servant set as a precondition that he will be the master? Who has ever seen anything like this? Who has even heard such utter nonsense?"

In telling all this to his friend who had also come to purchase a servant, he remarked mockingly, "In place of buying a slave, go purchase a master! For there is only one person up for sale, and I asked him about the type of work that he does, and in such a vein he answered me." Upon hearing these things, the friend thought, "Though it will startle most people, I shall go and look into him; for not without reason did the servant utter such words."

He approached the servant, who spoke as he had spoken to the first man. The friend asked him, "Why do you speak in this spirit, for you will find no one to purchase you." He answered, "That is so. I must inform you, though, that I come not from these lands but rather from a land that a foreign king conquered some time ago. The king treated the inhabitants of the land graciously; he spared their lives and allowed them to keep their money with them as they were brought to acknowledge his authority over them. And I went forth, dancing and rejoicing, without any money or possessions, naked just as you see me. The king was at the city gate observing all those leaving the city, each person with as heavy a burden as he could carry upon his shoulders. But when the king saw me among those departing, he noted that I was glad and joyous with nothing at all in my possession and no raiment upon my body.

"Then the king called to me and asked how it was possible that I had nothing at all to take out with me. I answered that I, too, was taking with me all that I had. Since no one sees what I have, I have no fear that anyone will take from me what I have. For truthfully it is at once both mine and not mine. And therefore, I will not deceive the one who comes to purchase me but will inform him of the service of which I am capable."

The man contemplating the purchase of a slave understood that this person was wise and faithful. He purchased him at a high price, appointed him as a person of authority and a patron over his entire household, and related to him as a master rather than as a servant. He ordered him to direct him and the other members of his household wisely, without favoritism or undue respect and to teach them wisdom and right conduct. And he commanded all the members of his household to serve him. For thus our sages had taught, and he had received the tradition from his fathers, "Serving a scholar is more important even than study."[1] For that reason they were all to submit themselves to his authority just as he himself, in seeing the man's faithfulness, would stand and serve him. For the servant had spoken truthfully and without deceit to any who came looking to purchase him.

And so it was that all the members of his household actually served him just as the master of the house did, and God prospered all that the master did in accord with the counsel of that wise man. All his possessions were subject to the authority of the servant, who rose higher and higher until he attained a very high position and became a person of renown. And his family endured for generations.

Now, on the following day, after that first man who stood by the trading block had spat in the servant's face and walked away from him, he, too, purchased a slave, one who claimed that he knew how to hunt and bring home prey. The owner valued his servant's talent, believing that the servant would surely make him rich, as each day he would hunt an animal or bird. The master would not only have food like a king but, in addition, would be able to sell the skins of the animals for profit.

With those considerations he purchased him and brought him home. He also purchased for him a sword and bow and as many arrows as he could carry. He told him, "Now, take your instruments and your bow and go out to the field to hunt for me and bring me food and prepare for me the tasty food that I love."[2] The servant went to the field and sat down under a tree to spread out his instruments and there he hunted some birds and fowl. But he thought, "What does it matter to me whether my master eats or not? Already the first day he has sent me to the field. I can tell him that I had no luck, and I'll slaughter those fowl and roast them here in the fire that I'll kindle from sticks I have gathered. I'll eat and be satiated, and I'll lie to him."

He did just as he had so contrived and he returned to the house empty-handed. The master, hearing his servant's explanation, considered it all plausible enough and did not pursue the matter. Rather, he gave him his portion of food as is customary to give to servants. And he sent him to purchase roast meat and other foodstuffs from the inn, and he ate.

Seeing this, the servant was quite pleased with himself for having already consumed what he had hunted. And he decided to do the same each day and, in addition, to steal silver and gold utensils from the master's house so that he might purchase white bread and aged wine. He would rise early in the morning and go out to the field—and just as he did that very first day, so he would do every day. "And it will suffice if once a month I bring him some dead animal that I happen to find." He did exactly as he planned, and he stole from his master whatever he wished.

He went out walking and sat down by a spring of water in the shade of a large tree, having brought with him various foodstuffs and drinks. He ate and slept and did not trouble to use his net or his bow. Sometimes, upon arriving back at the house, he feigned sadness over his ill-fortune in not finding anything to bring back to his master. Other times he told how he placed himself in great danger to combat a lion or a bear. In this way he directed his tongue, as a bow, at falsehood rather than at trustworthiness. And like a fool, the master believed everything he said, saying that it was all quite plausible. Meanwhile, each day, the servant stole his master's possessions and buried them beneath the ground in the field—until he had taken virtually everything in the master's house.

And out in the field he organized a band of companions who joined him in plundering passersby, until it happened that one of the robbery victims recognized the servant, knowing whose servant he was. That person went and informed the judges concerning all of the activities of the servant and his group of villainous friends in the field, reasoning that such actions could occur only with the consent and approval of his master. The judges called the master and informed him so that he might restrain his servant from further activity of this nature, for, if he did not, then the blame would be his.

When the master discussed this bad report with his servant, the latter, with the help of sweet talk and flattery, convincingly denied everything. The master's enemies, he explained, were seeking to shame him and so he should not take their charges at all seriously. The judges then proceeded to fulfill their responsibility, in the name of the law, to remove a danger from the population. They sent out spies who, it happened, verified more and more of those charges.

Again they spoke to the master, this time telling him that there were eyewitnesses and that the accusations concerning the servant were verified—"and if you are unwilling to restrain him, then it is clear that you yourself are guilty of those deeds, and when matters are brought to judgment, you will receive the same punishment as your servant receives." At this, the master merely laughed and made mockery of the judges. He responded that his servant was faithful and upright, even flawless in every respect, and that the whole accusation was but a lie, that in truth the one leveling such accusations against him was a thief and murderer. Upon hearing these words, the judges concluded that all the servant's actions were done with the knowledge of his master.

The people of his household would ask the master, "Why don't you believe the judges? They have no intent other than to assure the interests of order and justice in society. And we have observed with our own eyes that from the day this servant first came here, the house has slowly been emptied and that everything is deteriorating. So, if the judges say that the charges have been verified by eyewitnesses who confirm that he kidnaps and steals money, let them bring him to trial, and spare yourself."

But instead, the master arranged for advocates and attorneys to counter the judges and prove his servant's innocence. Even as the advocates and attorneys lied, the truth became ever more apparent to everyone, until the case was completed and both servant and master were found guilty of charges of unlawful conduct and plundering, violence, and deception.

The king was called upon to pronounce the sentence. And the master was very sad, for he finally admitted to himself that the judgment was true and just, and he regretted his attempts to deceive and to cover up what was obvious. But he could not change his position, for his actions in support of his servant were already public and written down for the record, and he had become an object of mockery and derision in everyone's eyes. The judges levied a heavy punishment on the master for defending and protecting his guilty servant, and whether he had done this knowingly or in ignorance, he shared in the guilt incurred as a result of the servant's deeds, which had brought injury to so many people.

And what caused him all this distress? Ignorance and pride—for he knew not how to distinguish between a wise man who speaks truth and between such a one as he had chosen—and because he did not purchase that first servant and serve him as one serves a master, as his friend had done.[3]

Mishnat ḥakhamim 311–313

1. Berakhot 7b.
2. Echoing Genesis 27:4.
3. While the author, Moses Hagiz, does not indicate the source or background of this tale, it would appear to reflect the Platonic view of animal appetite and reason, each competing within the human being for control of the whole person.

A Test

One cannot trust those willing to hurt themselves
in order to inflict pain and damage upon
another.

A wise king once sensed concerning two of his servants that one possessed the trait of envy and the other, that of desire and lust. He decided to test them in order to discover the true character of each.

And so as the two were standing together serving the king at his table and as wine fostered a merry mood in the king, he announced to them, "The time has come for each of you to request of me whatever you wish, and to the one who asks second I will give twice as much as I give to him who asks first."

In hearing the king's words and noting his magnanimous spirit, the envious one thought, "I will allow my comrade to ask first so that afterward I might receive twice as much as he." And, for the same reason, also the other one, the man of desire, remained silent and would not voice a request. After some time, out of his desire to hurt his comrade, the first one decided, in the wickedness of his heart, that he would make no request whatsoever of the king. But then in order further to hurt his fellow, he agreed to hurt himself in the process, and he requested that the king remove his right eye, so that the king would then remove both of his comrade's eyes.

The king then rebuked both of them as befits those with such evil traits. . . . And he sent them away saying, "Neither of you is worthy of serving me, for the day will come when one of you will envy me and the other will desire my queen. And I would be endangered because of your efforts to assume my place—though you must surely realize that, in so doing, you would also endanger yourselves."[1]

Mishnat ḥakhamim 489

Mishnat ḥakhamim places this parable within a discussion of the good heart, which, by its very nature, has no room for desire of that which belongs to another.

The Deceptive Island

One who is enticed by the pleasant things of life is
doomed to realize that they are fleeting.

A ship was sailing in the midst of the sea on its way to a distant land. The voyagers had lost their way and were wandering about at sea, hungry and thirsty, confined to the ship. They periodically caught sight of a large island there in the middle of the sea. It was the season when the trees were full of bright leaves, and on the island were to be seen all kinds of goodly trees and grasses and flowers, including roses and different varieties of violets. Sweet water was found on the beautiful and well-shaded island.

The ship's owner and the crew approached the island and disembarked to delight in its trees and rest in their shade. They ate from the fruit of the trees, drank the sweet water, and delighted in the sweet fragrance. They then left and returned to the ship to resume the voyage and find their way at sea.

One man among them decided not to leave even though the others pleaded vehemently with him, for he thought, "Where, anywhere else in the world, could I find such a place of delight, a paradise the likes of which even kings do not possess?" When they saw that he absolutely refused to leave, they continued on without him, found the sea route, and eventually reached their own land.

That one man remained there, eating of the island's fruits, drinking of the sweet water, and delighting in the marvelous fragrance of the spices. But when winter approached, the leaves of all the trees fell to the ground, as did their fruits and similarly all the spices. The springs also dried up. Only bare trees remained, affording him neither shade nor protection from either the dry hot days or the night frost. And he died there, hungry and empty-handed, having found nothing but untold distress.

So are we in this world like that ship sailing on the high seas. Like a lost ship at sea, we are unsure of our direction and know not to whom to turn or where we are going. In this world, which resembles such a sea, we discover a large island with all kinds of delights and pleasures, more than one can ever count.

There are those who—knowing the awe of God—partake of these pleasures in a limited way but then immediately return to God in repentance. They continue along their way, fulfilling God's will, even suffering the distresses of this world, which are like the agonies of being at sea, in order to proceed toward their place of rest. And, then, there are fools like that man who, so drawn to physical delights, remained to enjoy them until the season approached in which those delights ceased and in their place he found only bare trees and had neither food nor shade but only affliction and torment. This is the case with all those who follow the dictates of their eyes and the false desires of their hearts without considering what tomorrow will bring.

Kol sasson 1:9b

The motif of the ship and the island is found in several earlier sources, including: Joseph ben Judah, *Sefer musar*, ed. Wilhelm Bacher (Berlin, 1911), 20–21, no. 278; Isaac Aboab, *Menorat hameor* (Mantua, 1573), 89–90; and Al-Ghazali, *Moznei tsedek*, trans. Abraham ben Hasdai (Leipzig, 1839), 52–53, no. 7.

Good Dreams and Bad

*All pleasure can deceive except the joy of the soul
in eternity.*

There was a person in dire need of food, poverty-stricken to the point of illness and burdened by many debts. And at night he fell prey to worry. He dreamed that he possessed a million gold coins along with high rank, and he experienced tremendous and unbounded joy, for he was like a king seated at his royal table. But upon awakening he reached his hand into his pocket only to find it completely and hopelessly empty. All the next day he experienced distress and agony because of the very delight and joy of his dream—the wealth that he had seen in his dream turned out to be false, a mere lie. This left him even more agitated than before. It would have been far better for him had he never had that dream.

But if a man were to fall asleep at night and dream that someone close to him had died—or something worse than the usual agonies of this world—he would worry and panic and become dejected. But upon awakening and realizing that it was not true, that it was but a dream, how glad he would be! He would thank and praise the Creator just as though he had actually experienced such a distressful situation and was now released from it.

Similarly, a person's days and years in this world are like a dream. If one finds joy and delight in this world and all things go well for him, then when he awakens in the world of souls, he will know worry and sadness for, it turns out, it was all a lie and an illusion. . . . But if he had had a bad dream in that his days in this world were days of trouble and worry, then upon awakening he would be truly glad, for all that he had seen in his dream simply was not real.

Kol sasson 1:10b

The author of *Kol sasson* advocates linking the experience of worldly pleasures with the remembrance of death, when all joy and delight give way to sighing and distress. The only true state of pleasure, he emphasizes, is the soul's reward in the world of souls.

The Mission
and the Delays

Meeting the material needs of life is itself a holy
task insofar as it makes possible the fulfillment of
life's higher purposes.

A king sent his servant to a certain city concerning a particular matter. He made it clear that during that time the servant was not to occupy himself with anything else so as not to prolong his journey for any reasons except those related to his particular mission on behalf of his master.

While en route he met up with enemies, but with pleasant words he won their friendship and gave them food and drink. And he sat with them, feasting for an entire day before taking leave of them. He continued on to the ship in order to proceed with his mission, but the ship was foundering sliding in mud as can happen with ships when the water is too shallow. What did the servant do? He went about hiring some men to drag the ship from the mud; and they succeeded in moving it from its place. But in the process he lost a day. And, further, he met up with any number of similar situations, as can happen to a person on a journey, with the result that he lost several days.

Upon his return, even were the king to learn that his servant had had to spend many days in pursuits other than actual travel, he would still not be angered at him because of the delays, knowing that without those delays the man would have been unable to carry out the king's mission.

So it is that a person is sent to this world to fulfill a mission given by God. He is not sent to pursue any kind of worldly matters but rather to do His mitzvot and fulfill His teachings. Yet, were such a person not to eat or drink or engage in earning a livelihood, he would perish and die without ever fulfilling his Master's mitzvot.

Therefore, when he eats and drinks and sleeps with the intent of sustaining his body for the sake of being able to carry out the service of God, these activities themselves become as part of that divine mission and, hence, as part of the divine commandment.

Kol sasson 5:26b–27a

Life, including the satisfying of basic physical needs, is to be lived for the sake of God, according to the author of *Kol sasson*. One is not to eat, for example, for the sake of the pleasure involved. Rather, eating should be a means to a life of service to God, in which case the very act of eating is elevated to a level similar to that of Torah and the fulfillment of the divine commands.

We have come
to the end of a book
in which each of the stories
is a perception of life
as mirroring
that which is
beyond
appearances.

Bibliography

Aboab, Isaac, *Menorat hameor*. Mantua, 1573.

Abraham ben Isaac Hayyuth. *Sefer holekh tamim*. Cracow, 1634.

Alexander, Tamar. "Demuto shel haari basippur hasefaradi-yehudi," *Peamim* 26 (1986): 87–107.

Al-Ghazali. *Moznei tsedek*. Translated by Abraham ben Hasdai. Leipzig, 1839.

Al-Nakawa, Israel. *Menorat hamaor*. Edited by Hyman G. Enelow. 4 vols. New York, 1929–1934.

Assaf, Simhah. "Igeret nosefet shel rabi shelomoh shlumiel." *Kovets al yad,* n.s. 3 (1939): 120–121.

Avitsur, Shmuel. "Safed: Center for Textile Weaving in the Sixteenth Century" (in Hebrew). *Sefunot* 6 (1962): 41–69.

Band, Arnold J. *Nostalgia and Nightmare: A Study in the Fiction of S. Υ. Agnon*. Berkeley and Los Angeles, 1968.

Benayahu, Meir. *Sefer toledot haari*. Jerusalem, 1967.

Berdyczewski, M. J. *Mimekor yisrael*. Translated by I. M. Lask. 3 vols. Bloomington, 1976.

Bochner, Benjamin Zeev. *Or hadash*. Amsterdam, 1671.

Brody, Heinrich, ed. *Anthologica hebraica*. Leipzig, 1922.

Calloud, Jean. *Structural Analysis of Narrative*. Translated by Daniel Patte. Philadelphia, 1976.

Charles, Robert H. *The Apocrypha and the Pseudepigrapha of the Old Testament*. 2 vols. Oxford, 1913.

Cordovero, Moses. *Tomer devorah*. Venice, 1589.

———. *Pardes rimonim*. Cracow, 1592.

Culler, Jonathan. *Structuralist Poetics*. London, 1975.

Dan, Joseph. *Hasippur haivri bimei habenayim*. Jerusalem, 1974.

———. "Lekutot lemaasei 'nevuat hayeled.' " *Shalem* 1 (1974): 229–234.

———. "Letoldoteha shel 'Sifrut hashevahim.' " *Jerusalem Studies in Jewish Folklore* 1 (1981): 82–100.

———. "Sifrut hashevahim, mizrah uvmaarav." *Peamim* 26 (1986): 77–86.

————. *Jewish Mysticism and Jewish Ethics.* Philadelphia, Seattle, and London, 1986.

David, Abraham. "The Historical Work of Gedalya ibn Yahya, Author of 'Shalshelet hakabbalah.'" Ph.D. diss., Hebrew University, 1976.

Davidson, Israel. *Thesaurus of Medieval Hebrew Poetry.* 4 vols. New York, 1924–1933.

Delehaye, Hippolyte. *The Legends of the Saints.* New York, 1962.

Delmedigo, Joseph Solomon. *Sefer taalumot hokhmah.* Basel, 1629.

Eisenstein, Judah D., ed. *Otsar midrashim.* New York, 1915.

————. *Otsar massaot.* New York, 1926.

Elstein, J. "Predispozitsia ruhanit uparshanut hasippur hahasidi." *Bikoret ufarshanut* 18 (1983):43–68.

Farhi, Joseph S. *Oseh peleh.* Berlin, 1902.

Fine, Lawrence. *Safed Spirituality: Rules of Mystical Piety; The Beginning of Wisdom.* New York, Ramsey, Toronto, 1984.

————. "The Act of Metoposcopy: A Study in Isaac Luria's Charismatic Knowledge." *AJS Review* 11 (1986): 79–102.

Gaster, Moses. *The Exempla of the Rabbis.* Leipzig, London, 1924.

————. *Maaseh Buch.* 2 vols. Philadelphia, 1934.

Grunbaum, Max. *Neue Beiträge zur semitischen Sagenkunde.* Leiden, 1893.

Heschel, Abraham Joshua. *The Sabbath.* New York, 1951.

Horowitz, Isaiah. *Shenei luhot haberit.* Amsterdam, 1648.

Ibn Verga, Solomon. *Sefer shevet yehudah.* Jerusalem, 1947.

Isaac ben Samuel. *Sefer meirat enayim* (based on MS Parma 77). Jerusalem, 1975.

Jellinek, Adolf, ed. *Bet hamidrash.* 6 vols. Leipzig, 1853–1878; Jerusalem, 1938.

Joseph ben Judah. *Sefer musar.* Edited by Wilhelm Bacher. Berlin, 1911.

Kara, Avigdor. *Kodesh hilulim.* MS, Zentral-bibliotek, Zurich.

Kuhn, Peter. *Gottes Trauer und Klage in der rabbinischen Überlieferung.* Leiden, 1978.

Levi-Strauss, Claude. *Structural Anthropology.* Translated by Claire Jacobson and Brooke G. Schoepf. New York, 1963.

Loomis, C. Grant. *White Magic: An Introduction to the Folklore of Christian Legend.* Cambridge, Mass., 1948.

Maasiyot mitsadikei yesodei olam. Pedgorna, 1903.

Maasiyot umaamarim yekarim. Zhitomir, 1902.

Maranda, Pierre, and Elli Köngäs, eds. *Structural Analysis of Oral Tradition.* Philadelphia, 1971.

Menahem Azariah Fano. *Kanfei yonah.* Karatz, 1786.

Midrash tanhuma. Edited by Solomon Buber. New York, 1946.

Najara, Israel. *Sefer keli mahazik berakhah.* Constantinople, 1734.

Orhot hayyim. Prague, 1612.

Poppers, Meir. *Or zaddikim*. Hamburg, 1690.

Prince, Gerald. *Narratology: The Forms and Functioning of Narrative*. Berlin, New York, Amsterdam, 1982.

Propp, Vladimir. *Morphology of the Folktale*. Austin, 1973.

Robinson, Ira. "Messianic Prayer Vigils in Jerusalem in the Early Sixteenth Century." *Jewish Quarterly Review* 72 (1981): 32–42.

Roth, Cecil. *History of the Jews of Italy*. Philadelphia, 1946.

Rozanes, Salomon. *Korot hayehudim beturkiah veartsot hakedem*. 5 vols. Sofia, 1938.

Ruderman, David. "Three Contemporary Perceptions of a Polish Wunderkind of the Seventeenth Century." *AJS Review* 4 (1979): 143–164.

Schechter, Solomon. "Safed in the Sixteenth Century: A City of Legists and Mystics." In *Studies in Judaism: Second Series*. Philadelphia, 1908.

Scholem, Gershom. "Rabi avraham ben eliezer halevi." *Kiriat Sefer* 2 (1925–1926): 101–141, and 7 (1930–1934): 149–165.

———. "Shtar hahitkashrut shel talmidei haari." *Zion* 5 (1940): 125, 241ff.

———. *Major Trends in Jewish Mysticism*. New York, 1946.

———. "Shir shel yisrael najara befi hashabtaim." In *Ignace Goldziher Memorial Volume*, edited by Samuel Löwinger and Joseph Somogyi. Vol. 1. Budapest, 1948.

———. Response to A. Yaari (in Hebrew). *Behinot bevikoret uvesifrut* 8 (1955): 79–95, and 9 (1956): 80–84.

———. "Mekorotav shel 'Maase rabi gadiel hatinok' besifrut hakabbalah." In *Leagnon Shai*, edited by Dov Sadan and Efraim E. Urbach. Jerusalem, 1959.

———. *On the Kabbalah and Its Symbolism*. Translated by Ralph Manheim. New York, 1965.

———. *Kabbalah*. Jerusalem, 1974.

Scholes, Robert. *Structuralism in Literature*. New Haven, 1974.

Seder megilat ekha utefilat lel tishah beav ukinot keminhag ashkenazim upolin. Mantua, 1720.

Sefer hakavanot umaase nissim. Constantinople, 1720.

Sefer tsefat. Edited by Yitshak Ben-Zvi and Meir Benayahu. *Sefunot* 6–7 (1962–1963).

Shivhei haari. Lvov, 1849.

Strauss, Eli. *Toledot hayehudim bemitsrayim vesuriah tahat shilton hamamlukim*. Jerusalem, 1960.

Tamar, David. "The Ari and Rabbi Hayyim Vital as Messiah Son of Joseph" (in Hebrew). *Sefunot* 7 (1963): 169–177.

———. *Mehkarim betoledot hayehudim beerets yisrael uveitaliah*. Jerusalem, 1970.

———. *Bikoret umasa, ishim usefarim*. Jerusalem, 1973.

Tana devei eliyahu. 2 vols. Jerusalem, 1959.

Thompson, Stith. *Motif-Index of Folk-Literature.* Helsinki, 1932–1936; Bloomington, 1955.

Tishby, Isaiah. *Mishnat hazohar.* Vol. 1, with P. Lachover. Jerusalem, 1949; Vol. 2. Jerusalem, 1961.

————. *Netivei emunah uminut.* Ramat Gan, 1964.

————. "Hanhagot natan haazati, igarot rabi mosheh zakhut vetakanot rabi hayyim abulafia besefer *Hemdat yamim.*" *Kiriat Sefer* 54 (1979): 585–610.

Urbach, Efraim E. *Hazal: Pirkei emunot vedeot.* Jerusalem, 1969.

Vital, Hayyim. *Sefer hahezionot.* Edited by Aharon Z. Eshkoli. Jerusalem, 1954.

Werblowsky, R. J. Zwi. *Joseph Karo: Lawyer and Mystic.* Oxford, 1962.

Wineman, Aryeh. *Aggadah veomanut: Iyunim beyetsirat agnon.* Jerusalem, 1982.

————. "Hakham and Hasid: The Paradoxical Story in the Kabbalistic Ethical Literature." *Hebrew Studies* 25 (1984): 52–61.

————. "The Dialectic of *Tikkun* in the Legends of the Ari." *Prooftexts* (1985): 33–44.

————. "The Metamorphosis of Narrative Traditions: Two Stories from Sixteenth-Century Safed." *AJS Review* 10 (1985): 165–180.

Yaari, Abraham. *Taalumat sefer.* Jerusalem, 1954.

————. *Iggarot erets yisrael.* Ramat Gan, 1971.

The Zohar. Translated by Harry Sperling and Maurice Simon. 5 vols. London, 1931–1934.

Zohar: The Book of Enlightenment. Translated by Daniel Matt. New York, Ramsey, Toronto, 1983.